To two of the
people we know,

Jeanne &
Nicholas

THE NEW YORKER

BOOK OF ALL~NEW CAT CARTOONS

THE NEW YORKER
BOOK OF ALL~NEW CAT CARTOONS

ALFRED A. KNOPF ❧ NEW YORK 2003

THIS IS A BORZOI BOOK
PUBLISHED BY ALFRED A. KNOPF, INC.

ISBN 0-375-40108-3
LC 97-80685

Manufactured in the United States of America
Published December 19, 1997
Reprinted Once
Third Printing, April 2003

THE
NEW YORKER
BOOK OF ALL~NEW CAT CARTOONS

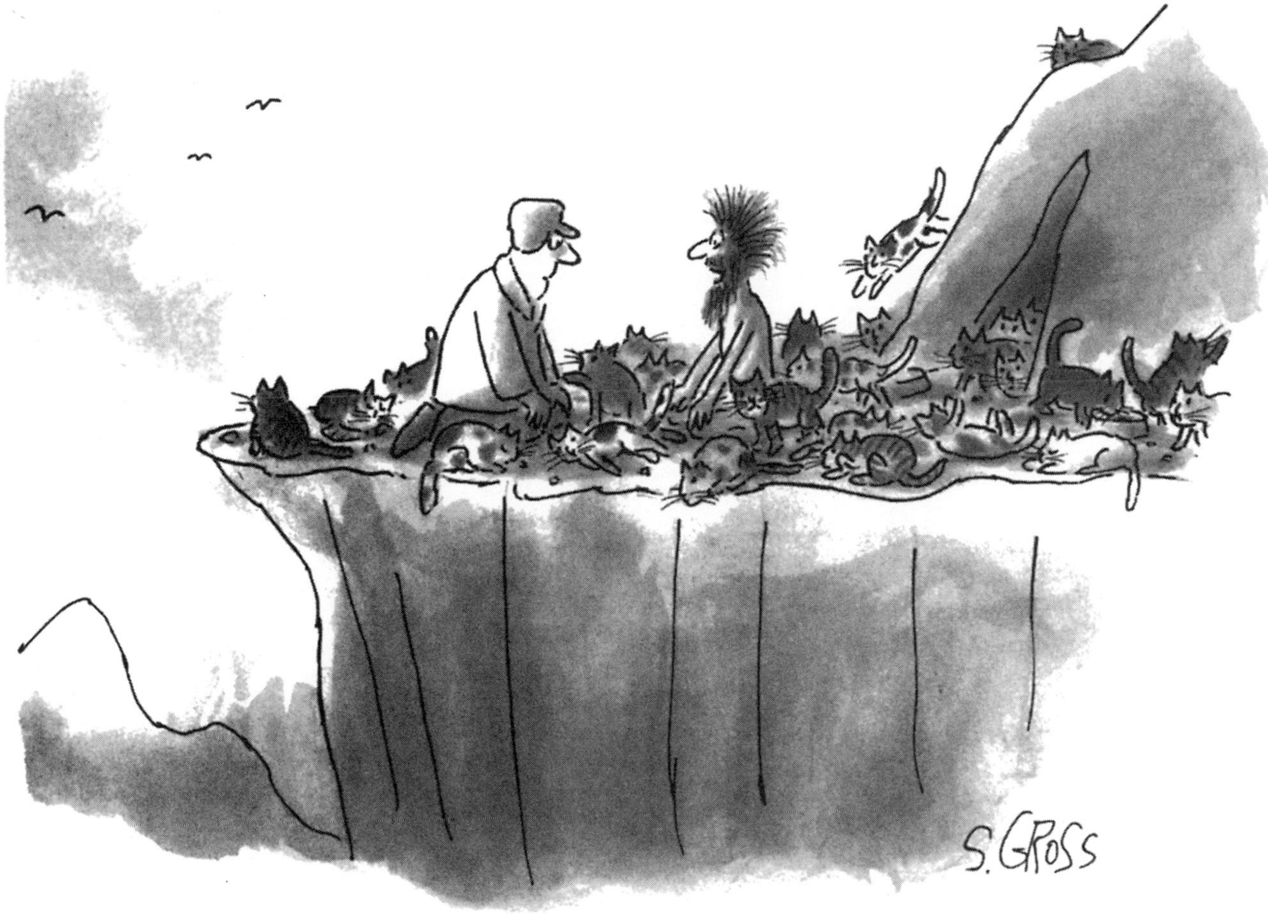
S. GROSS

"The meaning of life is cats."

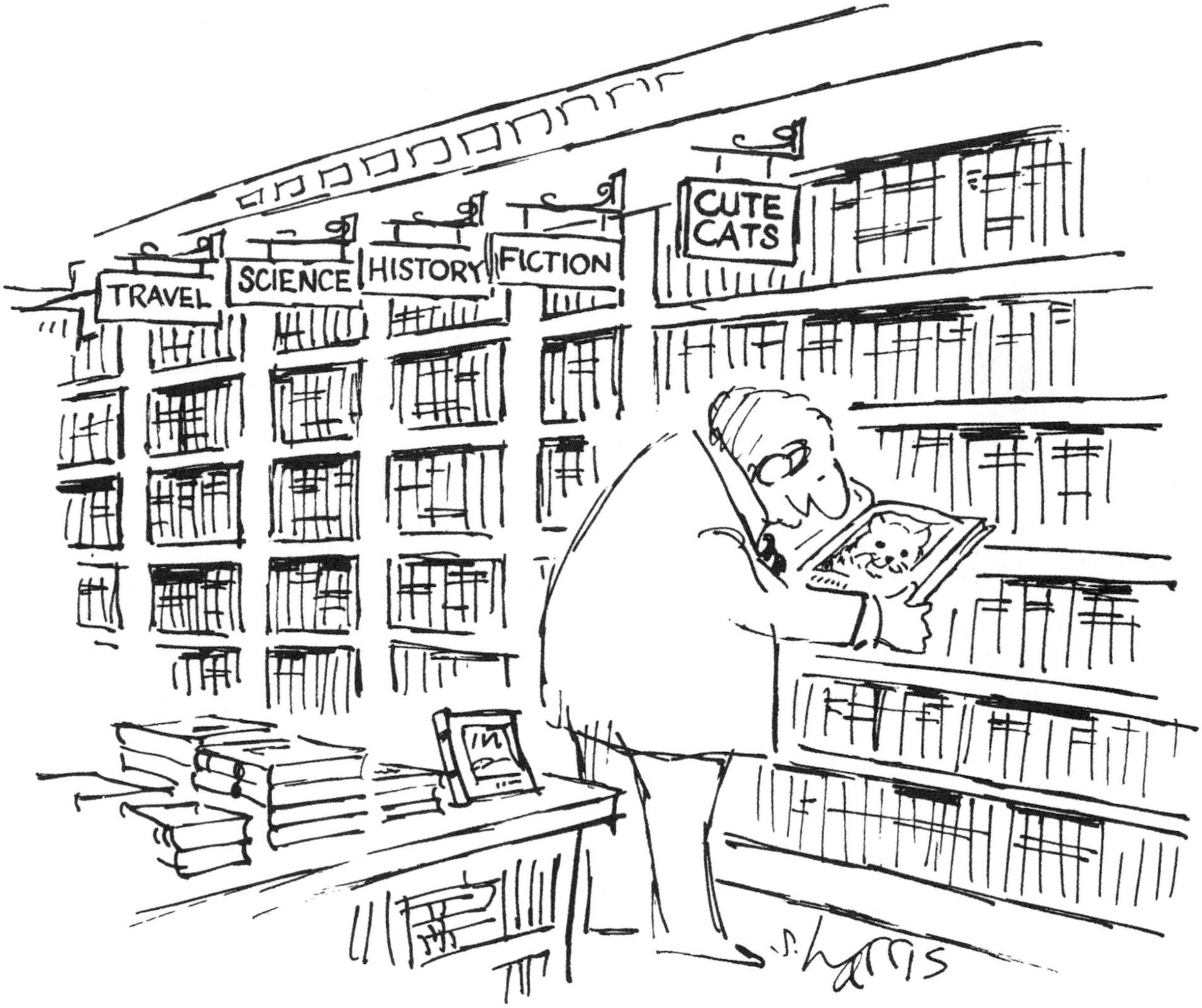
TRAVEL
SCIENCE
HISTORY
FICTION
CUTE CATS
S. Harris

"I tell you, the book has everything—sex, history, consciousness, and cats!"

DOG DAYS

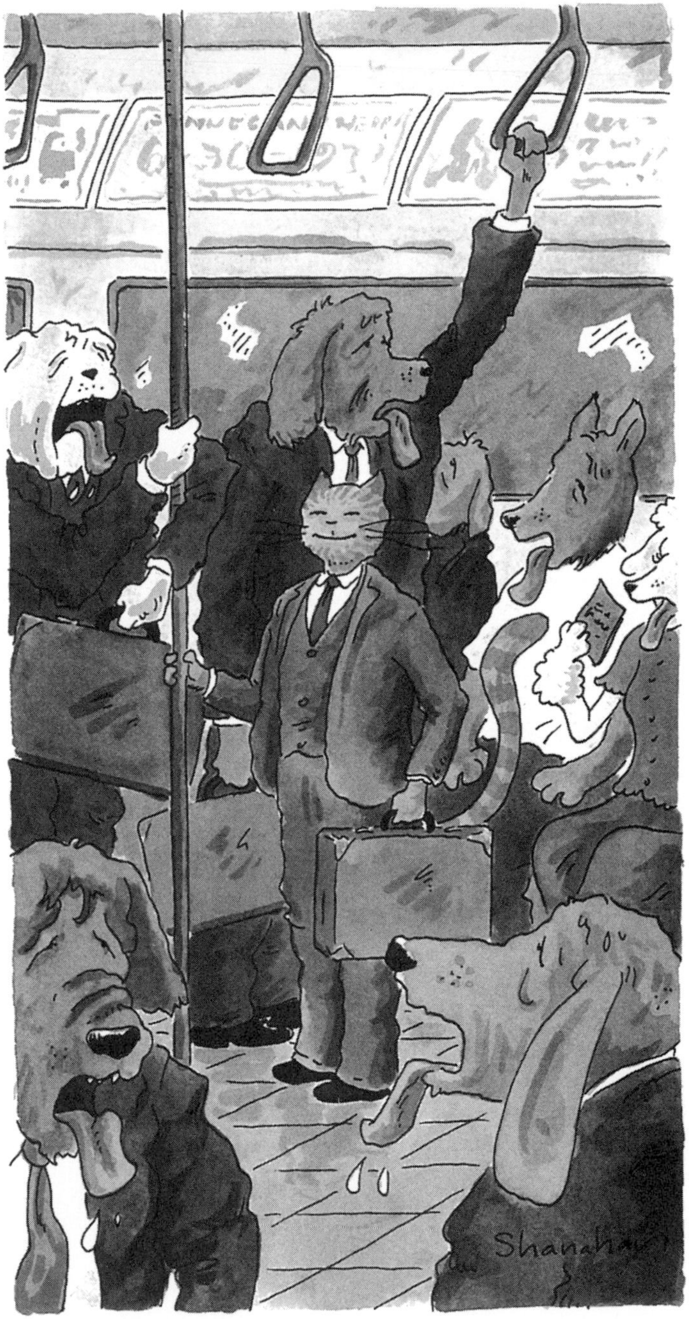
Shanahan

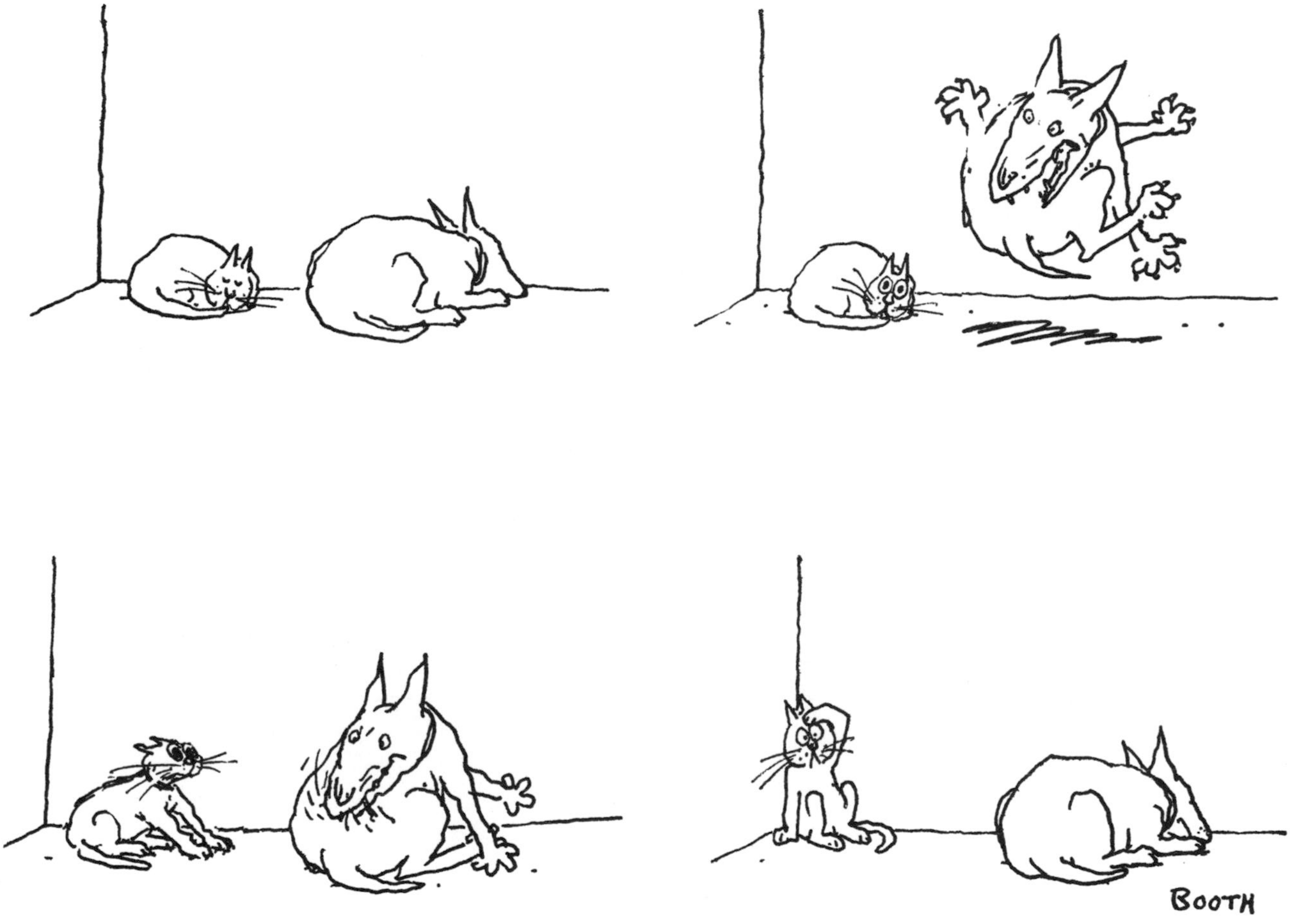
BOOTH

GREAT MOMENTS IN MUSIC

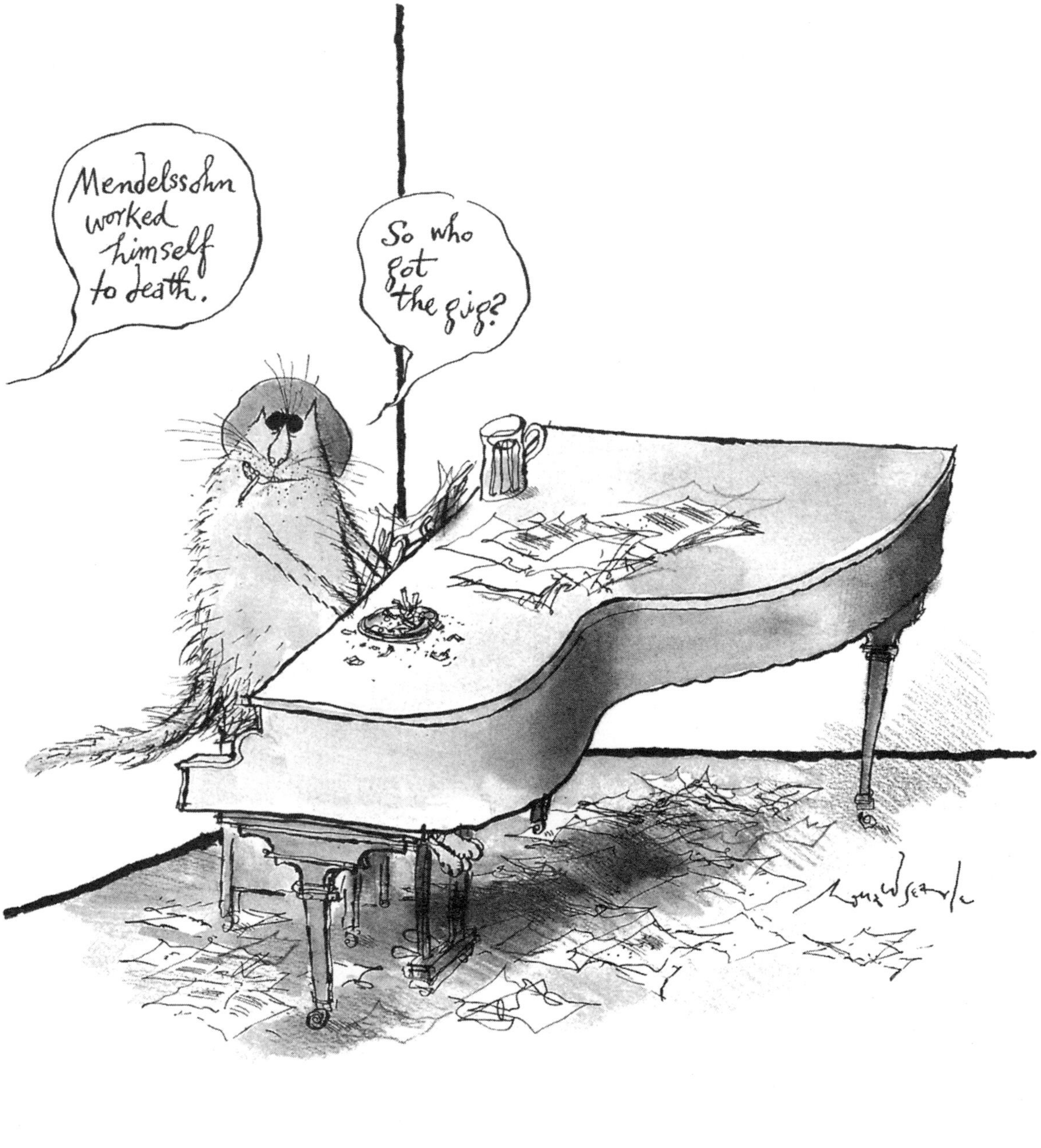
Mendelssohn worked himself to death.
So who got the gig?

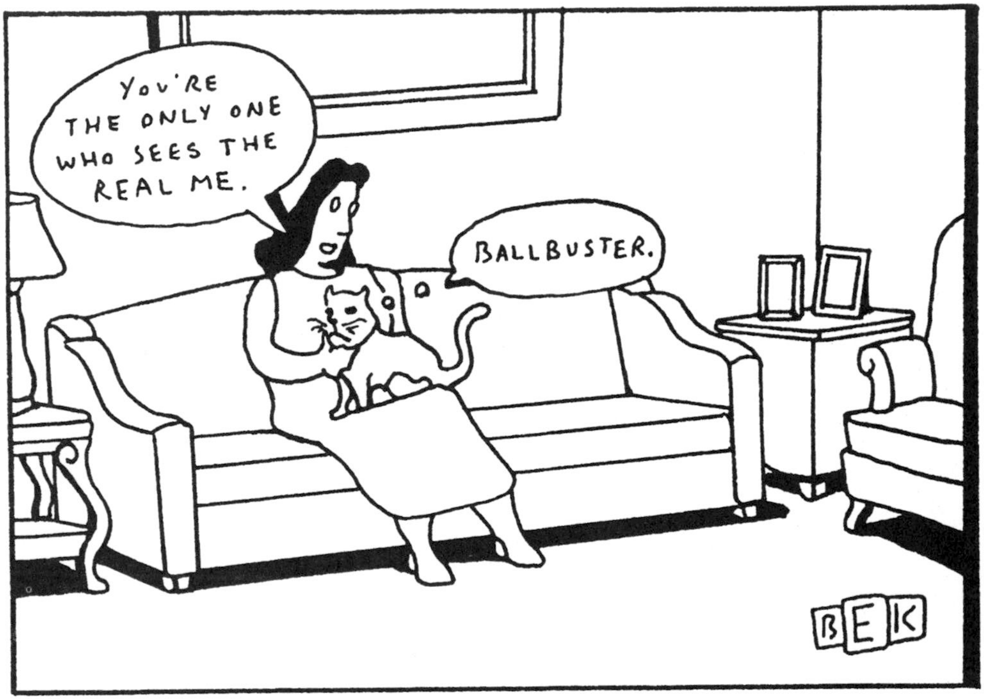
YOU'RE THE ONLY ONE WHO SEES THE REAL ME.
BALLBUSTER.
BEK

ALTERNATIVE DICKENS

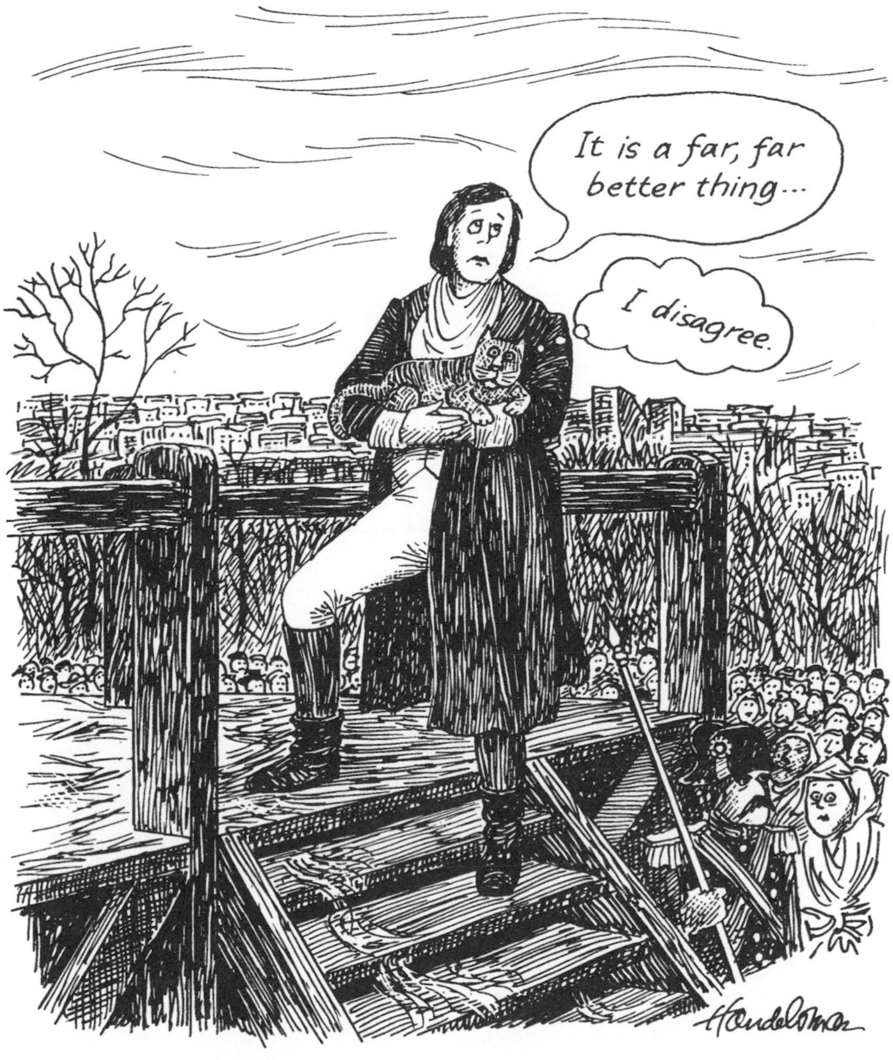
It is a far, far better thing...
I disagree.
Handelsman

SYDNEY CARTON REFUSES TO GO TO THE GUILLOTINE WITHOUT HIS CAT.

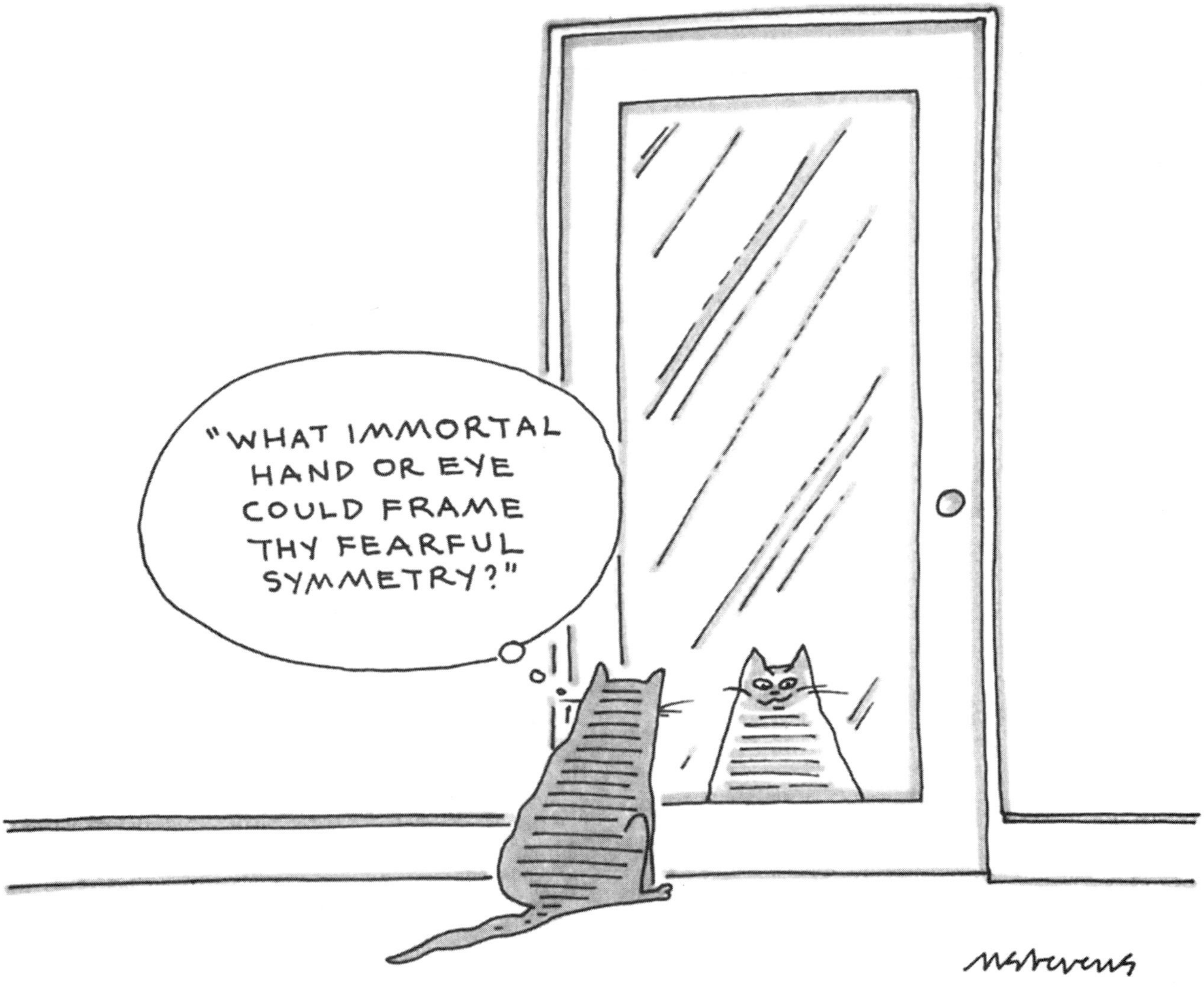
"WHAT IMMORTAL HAND OR EYE COULD FRAME THY FEARFUL SYMMETRY?"

"That one is Marvin's personal pussycat."

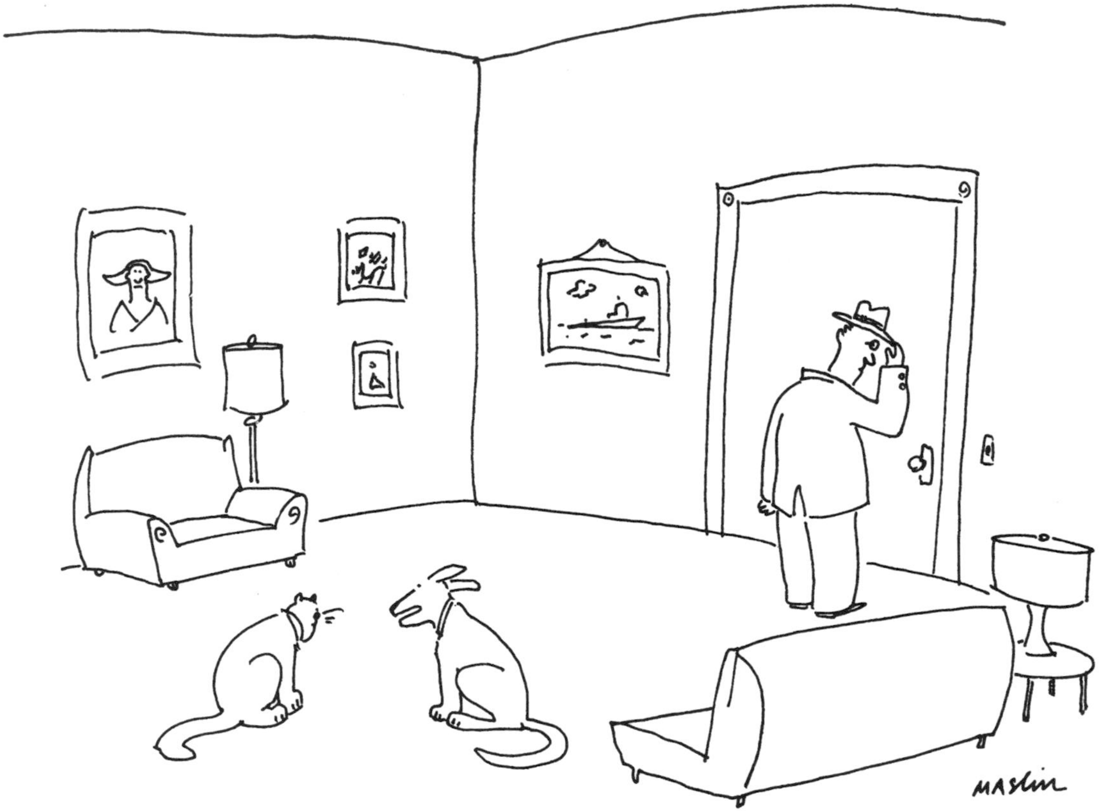
MASLIN

"When he leaves, I'm in charge."

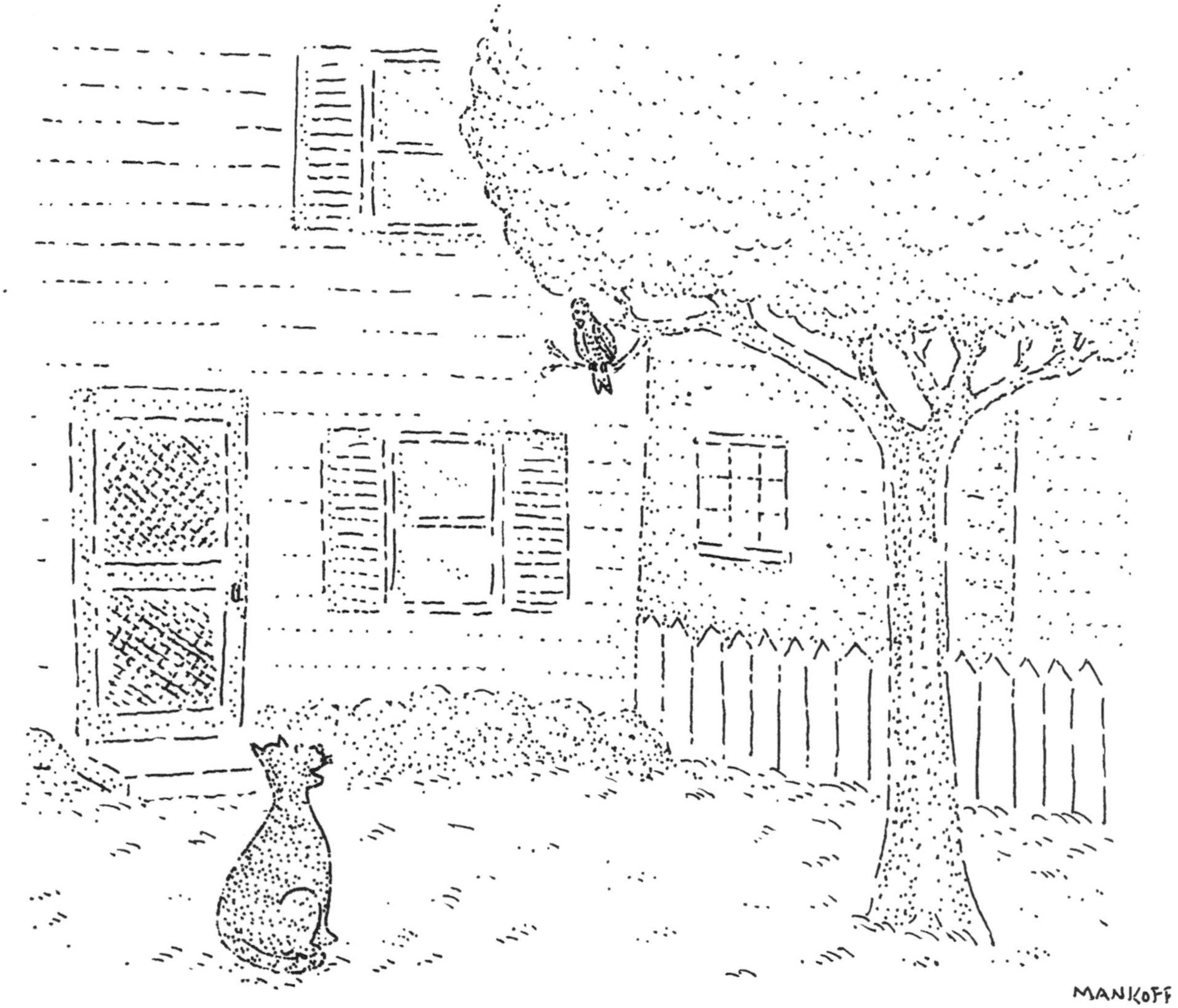
MANKOFF

"Hey, let's do lunch."

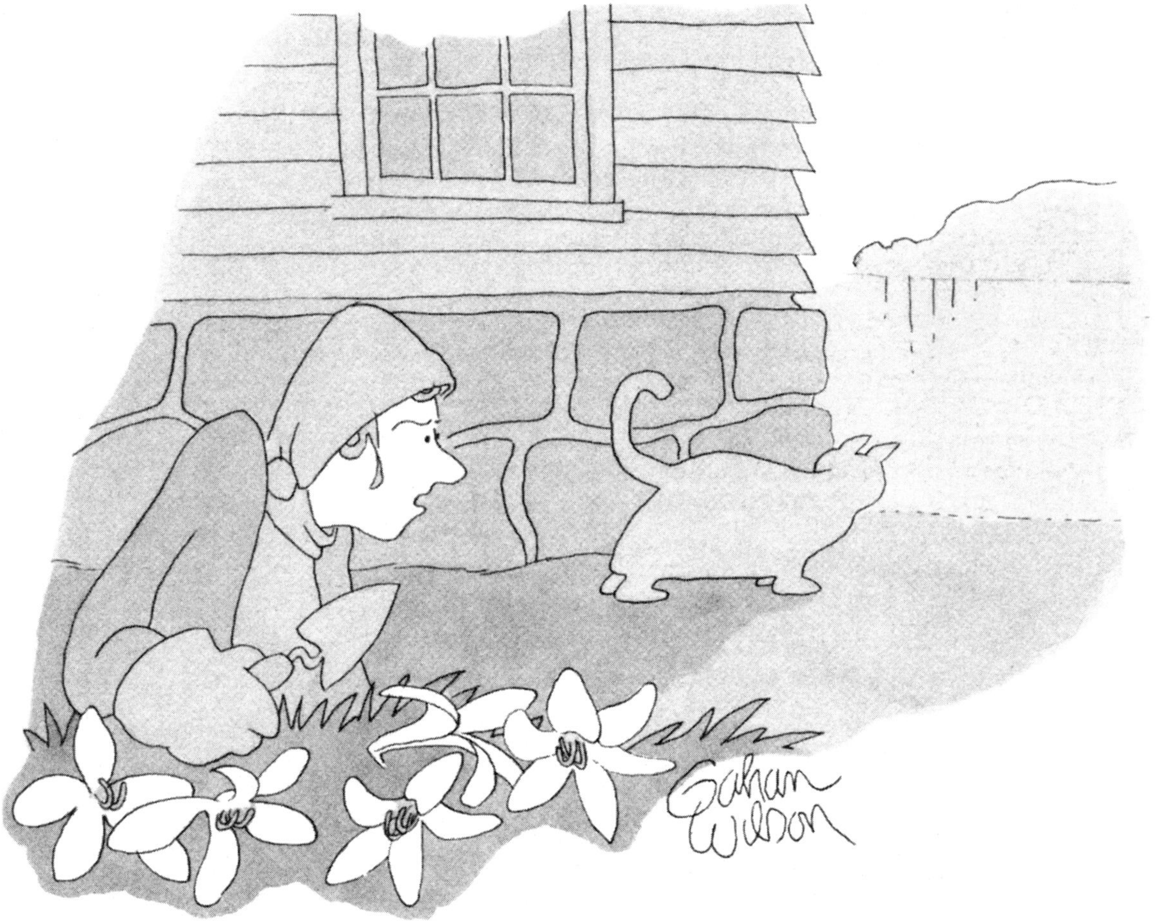
Gahan Wilson

"Just what do you think you're up to?"

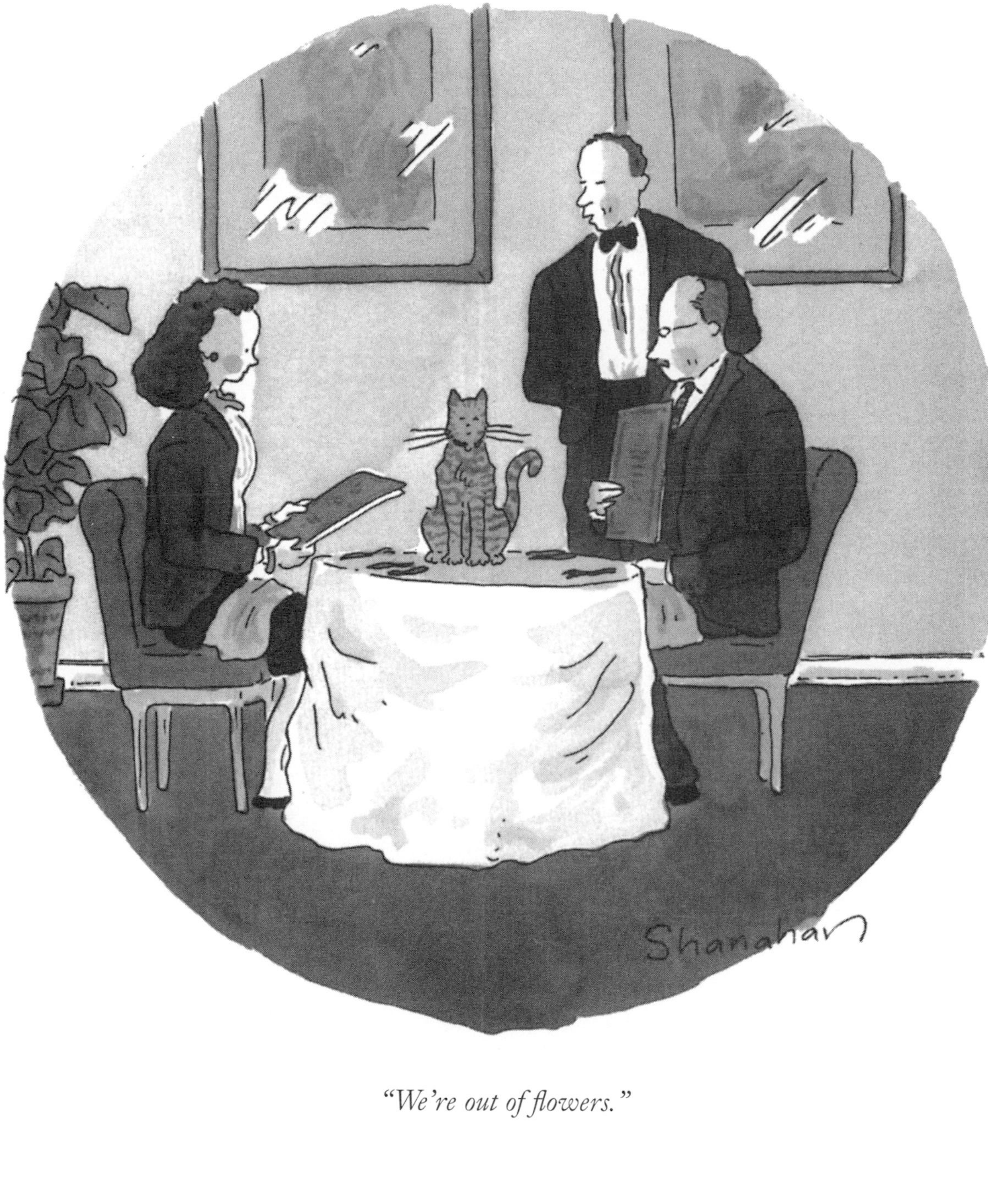
Shanahan

"We're out of flowers."

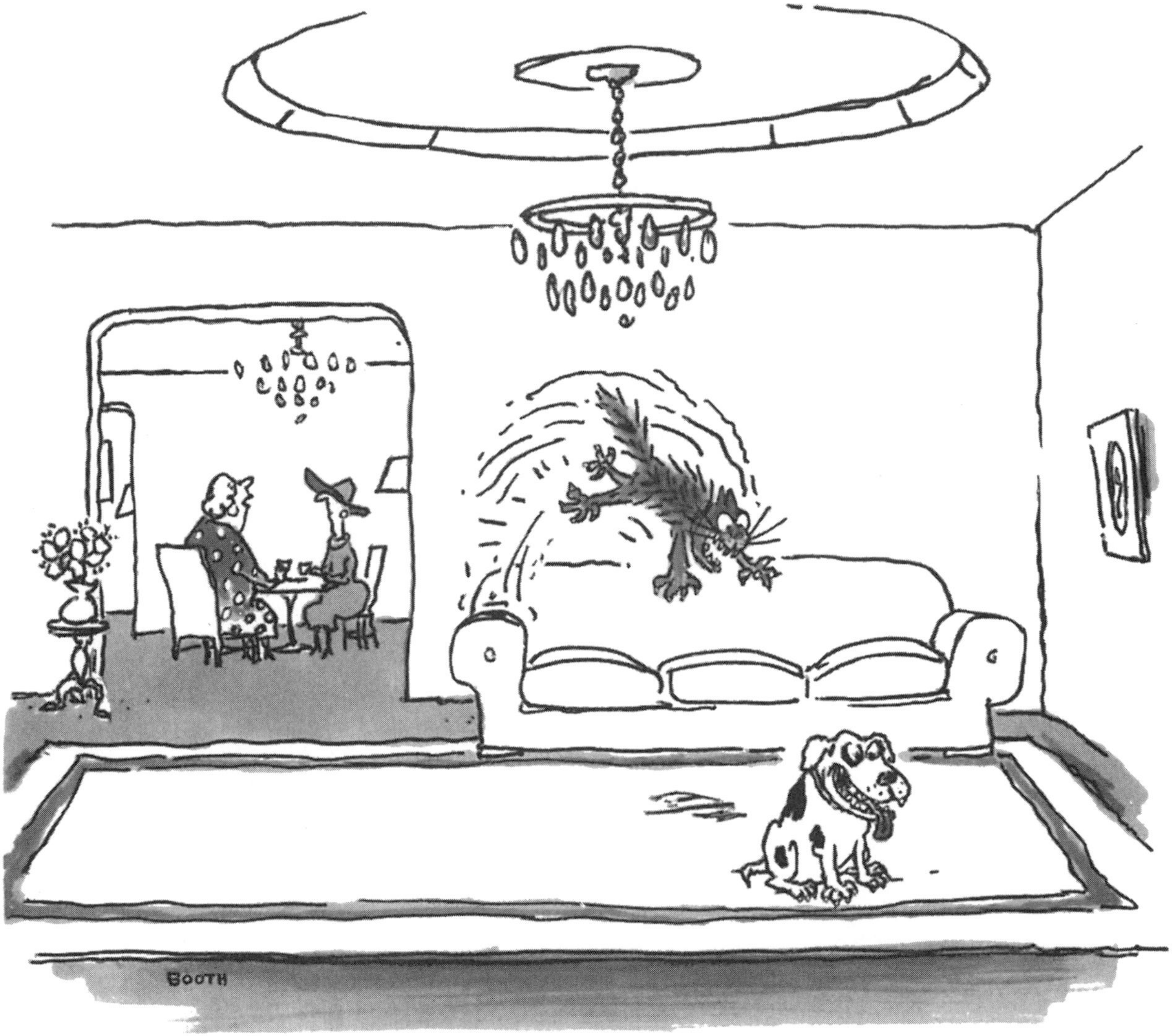
BOOTH

"I feed the cat nothing but veggies."

NO!
TRY IT!
S. GROSS

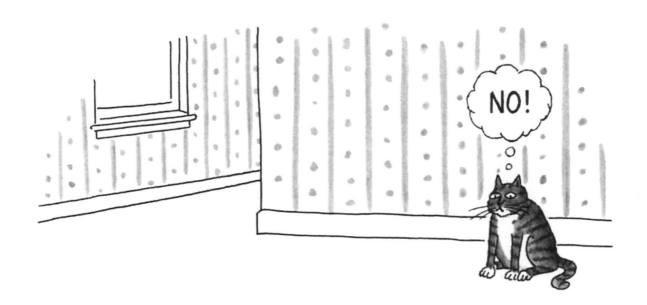

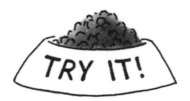

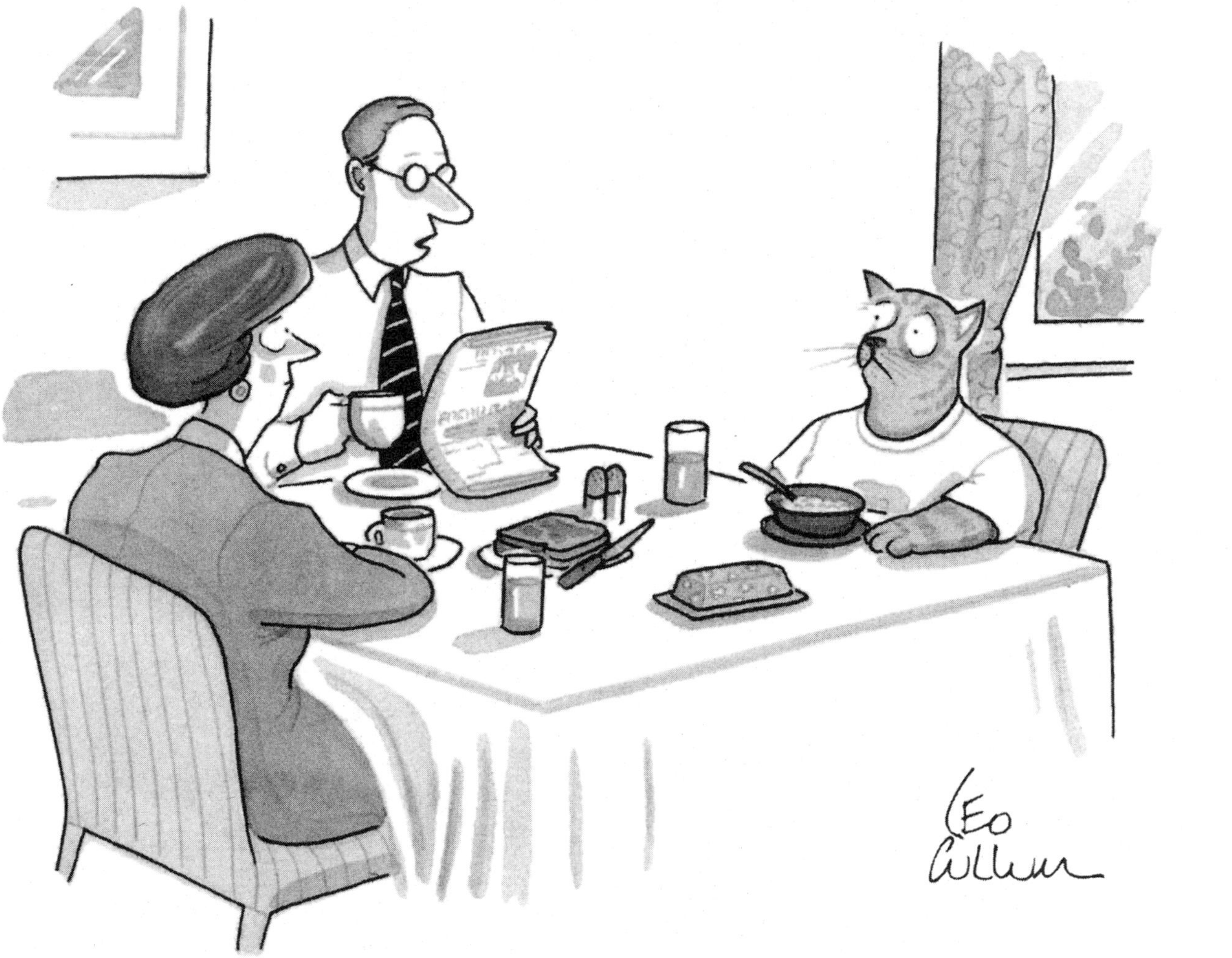

"If you must know, Jimmy, you came from a box in front of the market. It said 'Free Kittens.'"

JOSEPH
FARRIS

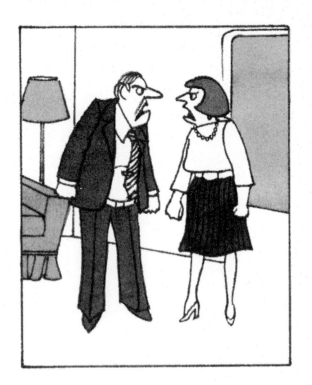

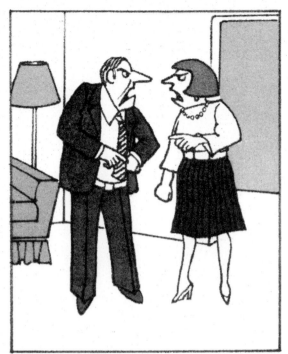

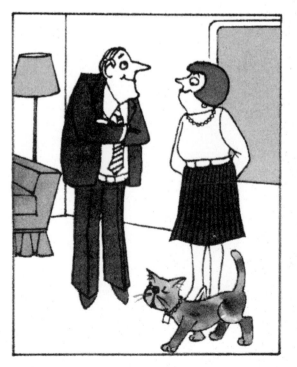

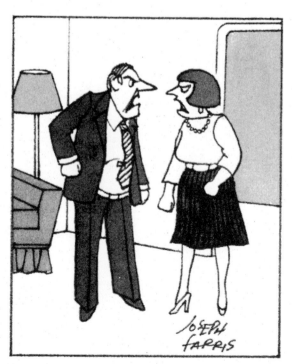

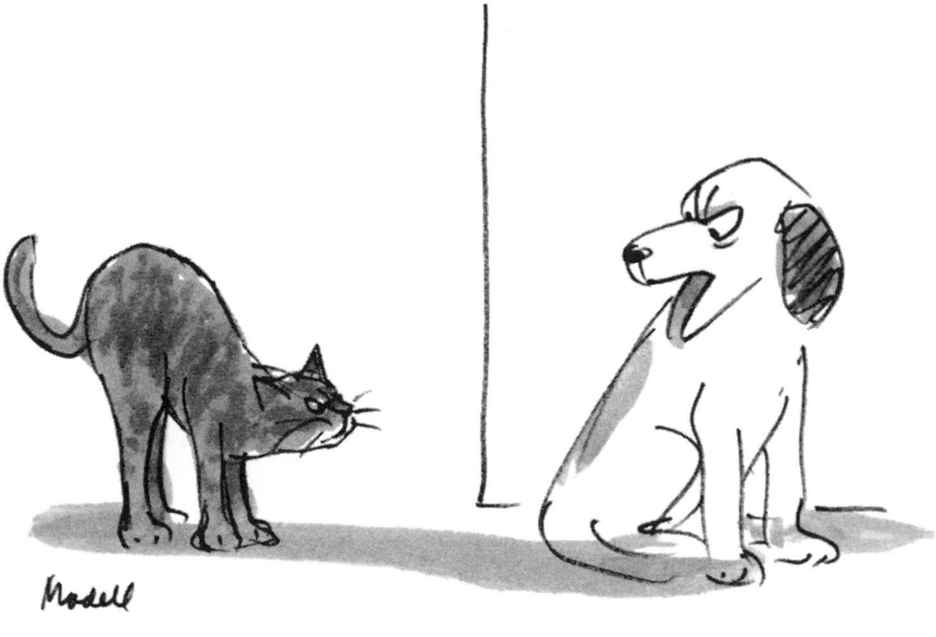
Modell

"What is it with you, anyway?"

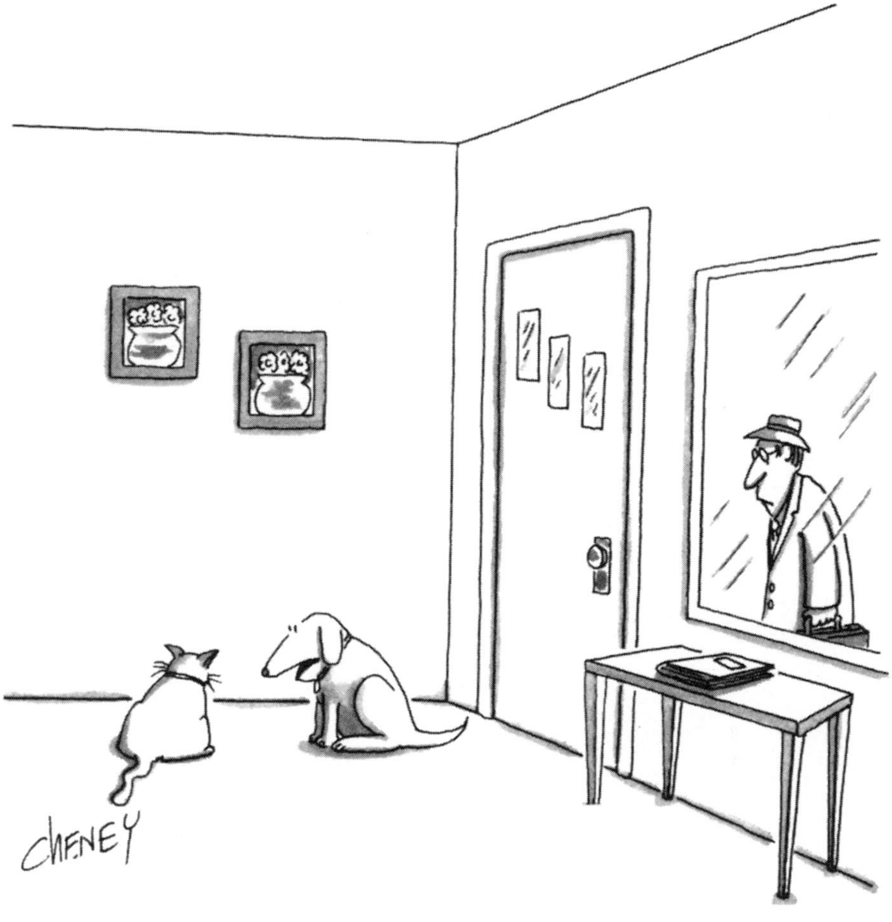
CHENEY

*"He's my best friend and he works hard all day.
Couldn't you at least wag your tail?"*

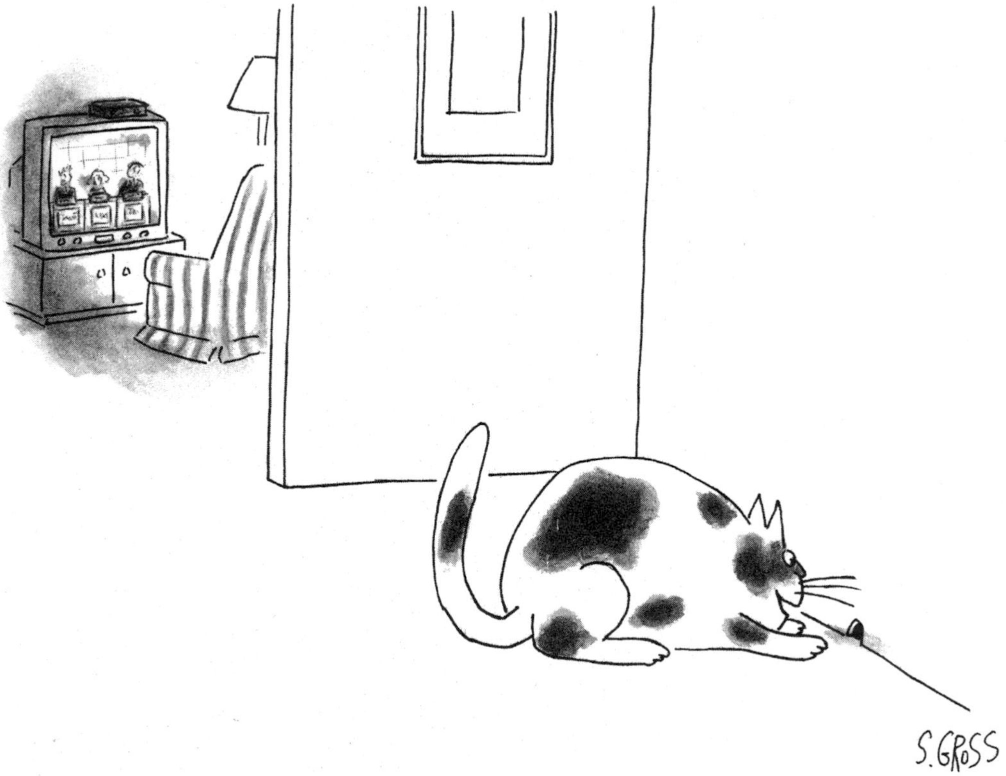
S.GROSS

"*Jeopardy!* is on."

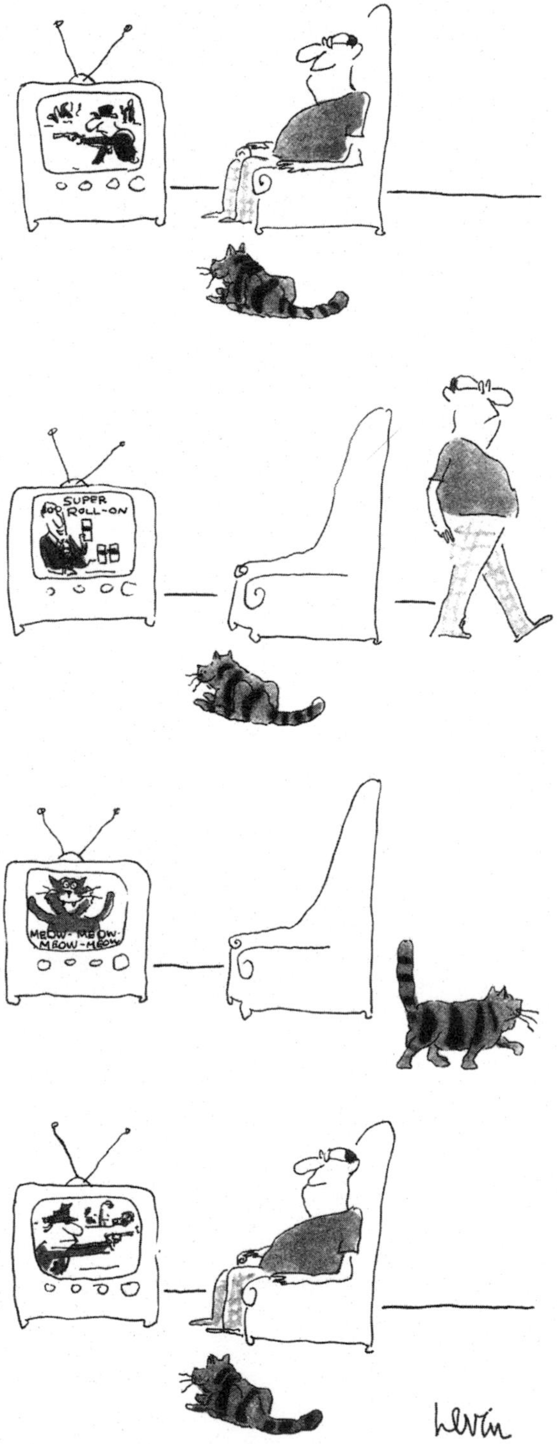
SUPER
ROLL-ON
MEOW- MEOW-
MEOW-MEOW
Levin

Second thoughts

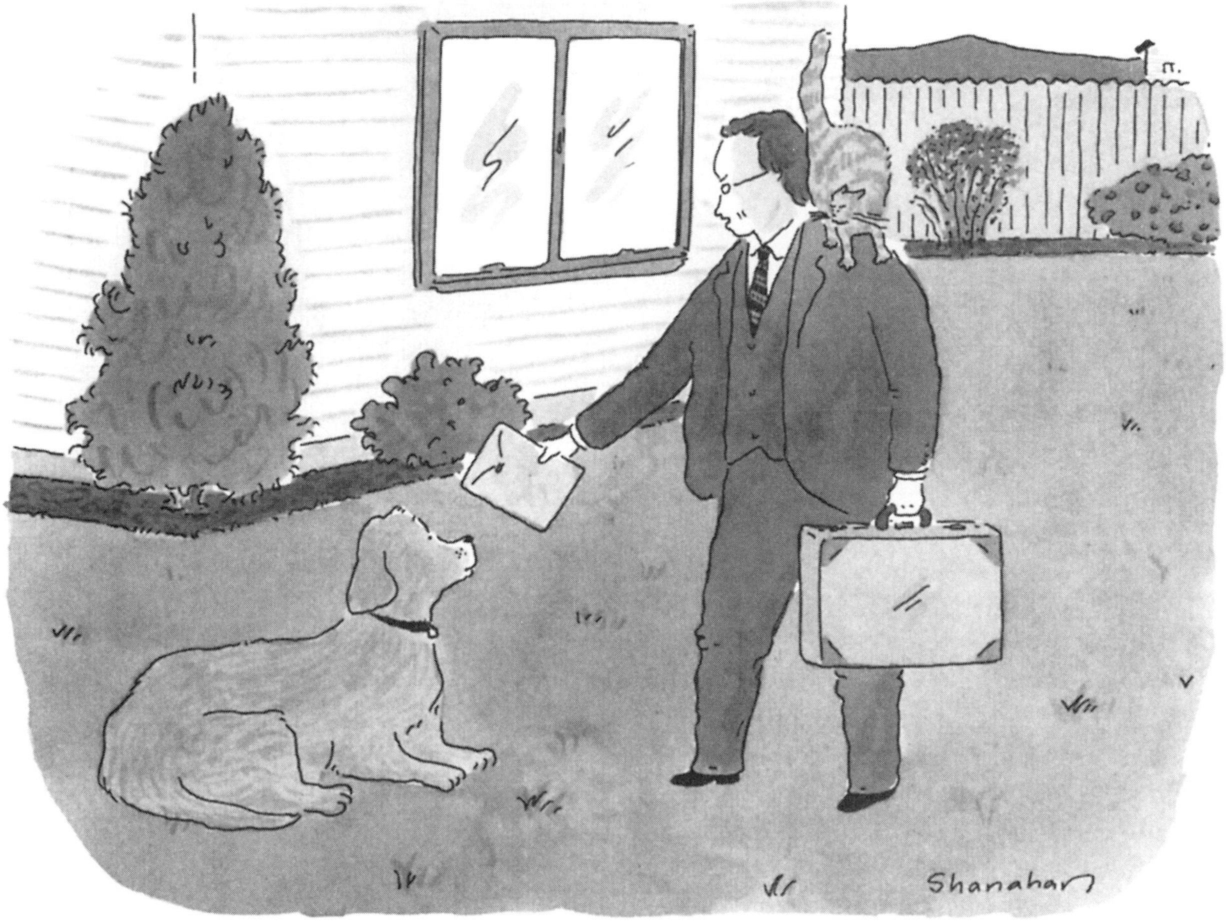
Shanahan

"We're slapping you with a stress suit, pal!"

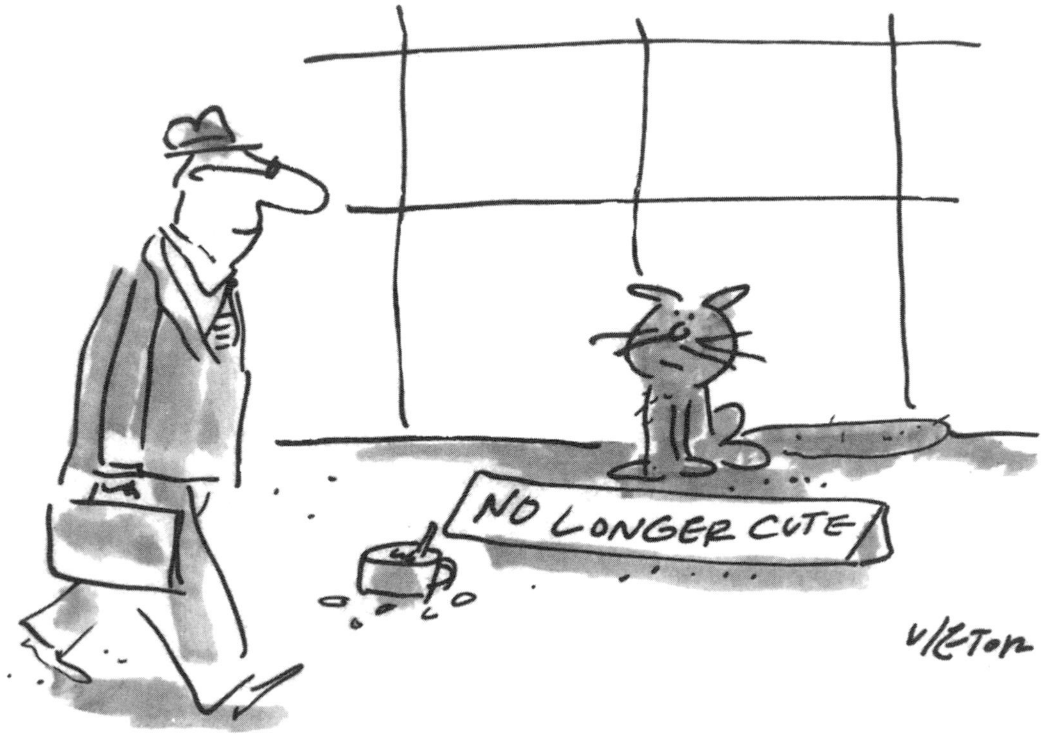
NO LONGER CUTE
VICTOR

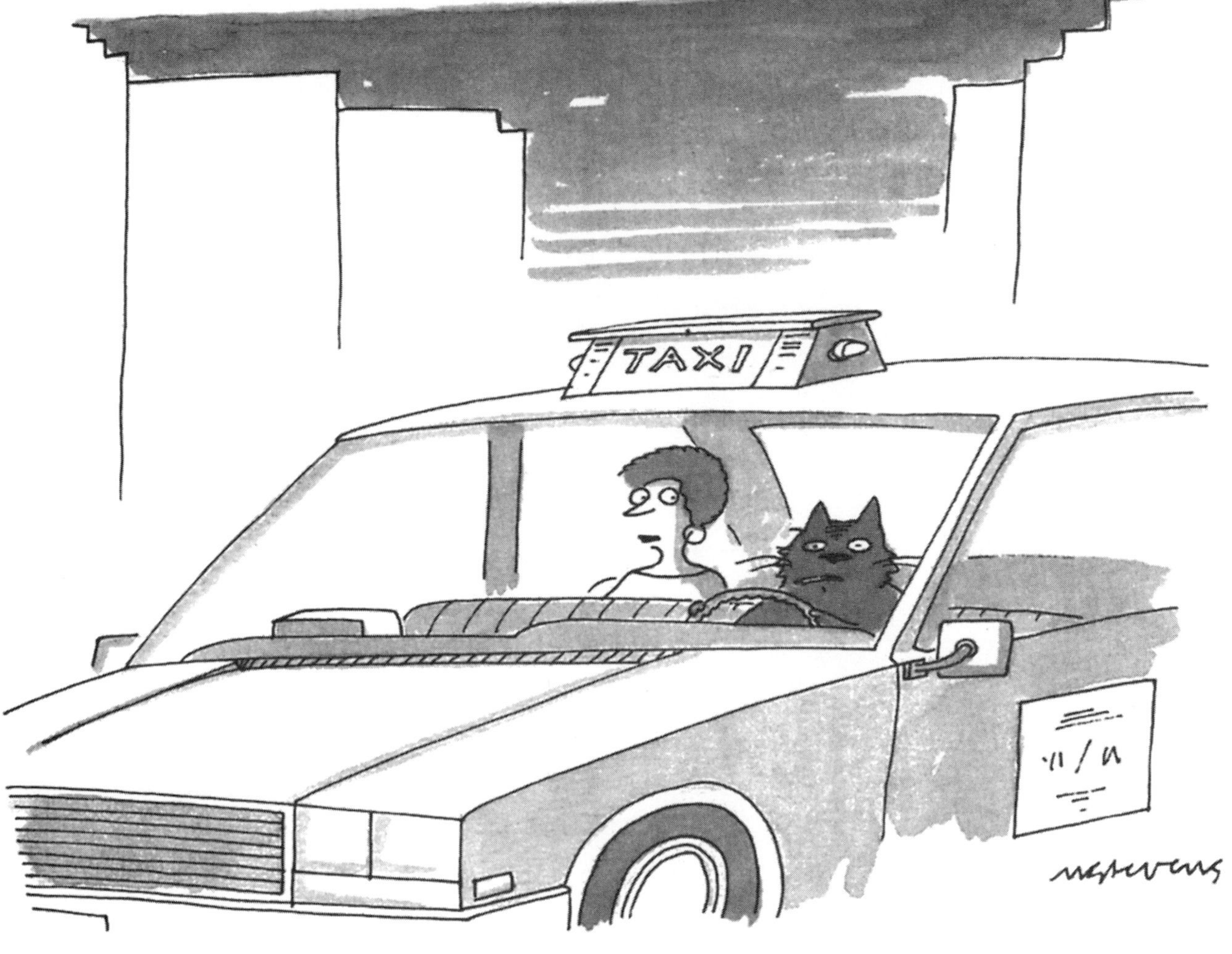
TAXI

"Yeah, I was into the pet thing for a while, but that scene wasn't for me."

"*You never chase me through back yards anymore.*"

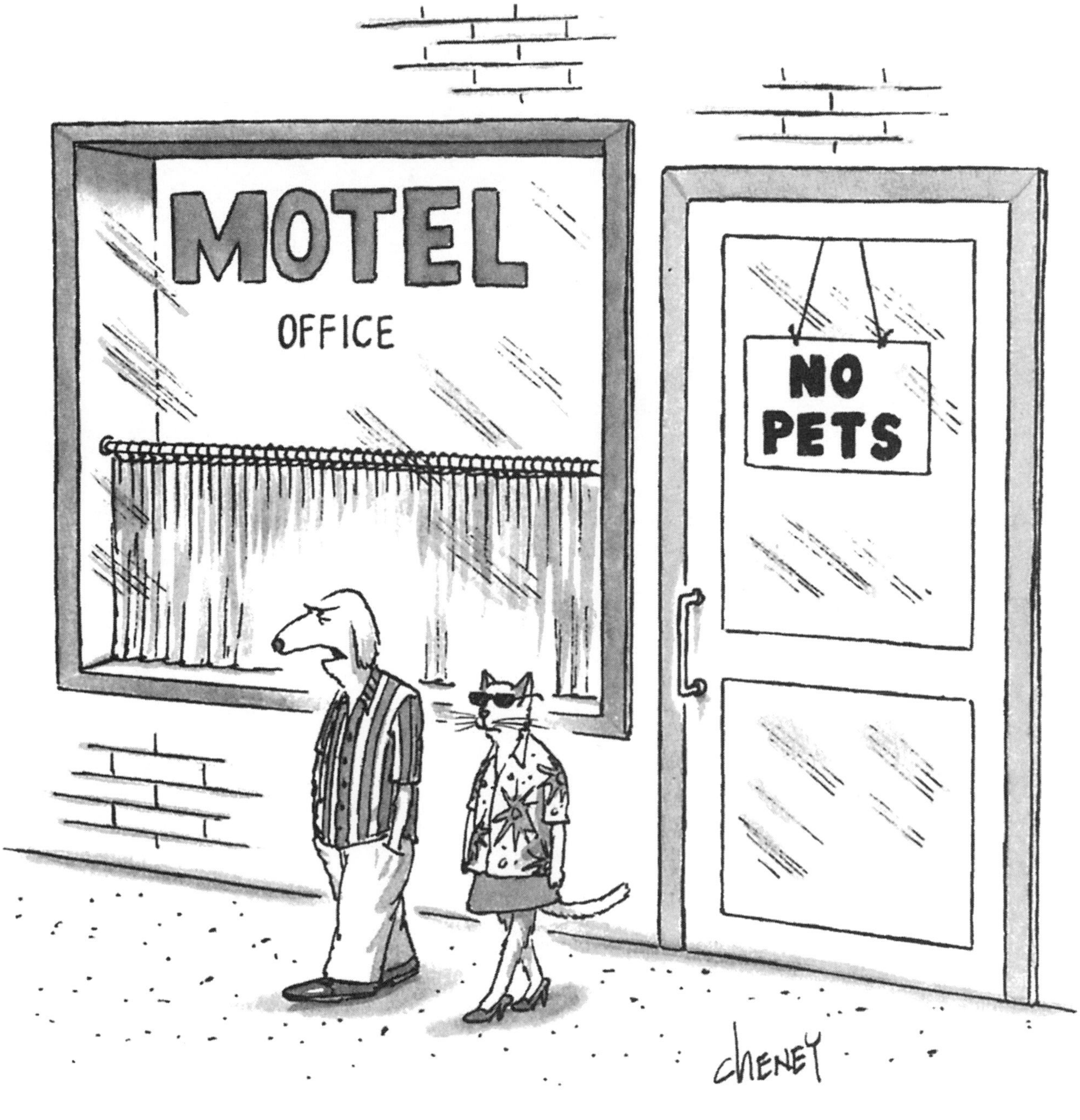
MOTEL
OFFICE
NO
PETS
cheney

"I can't believe it! I had the key right in my paw, and you had to cough up a hairball!"

Is Your Cat on Drugs?
Look For These Warning Signs-
Has a torrid affair with your favorite mohair sweater.
Plays Mötley Crüe tape backward.
Refuses to play with rubber mouse.
Has telltale catnip breath.
Would rather eat sugar-coated breakfast cereal than kitty bits.
FLUFFO
SKALISKY

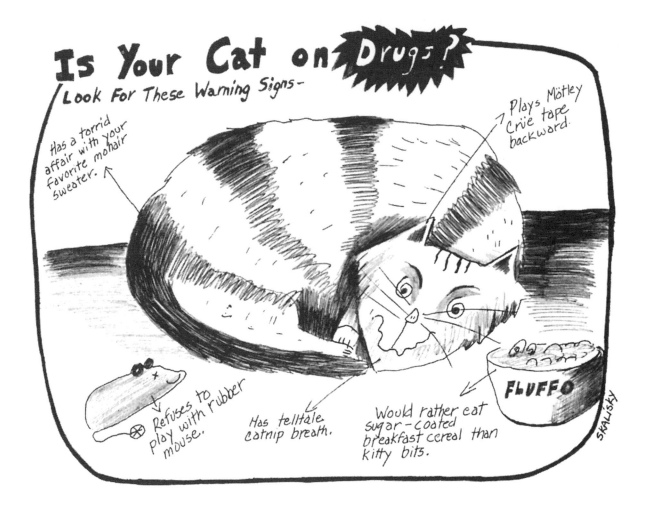

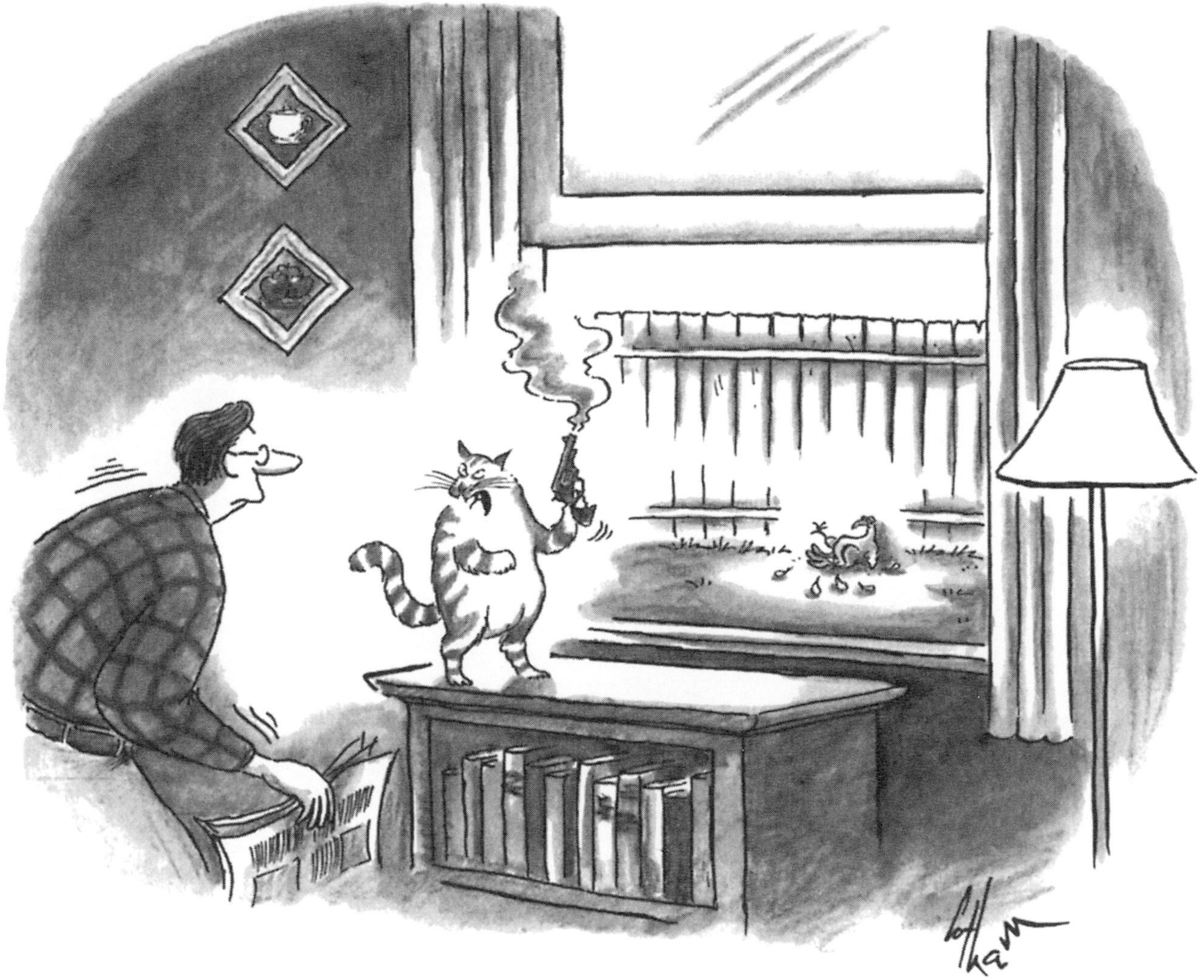

"What the hell was I supposed to do? I've been declawed!"

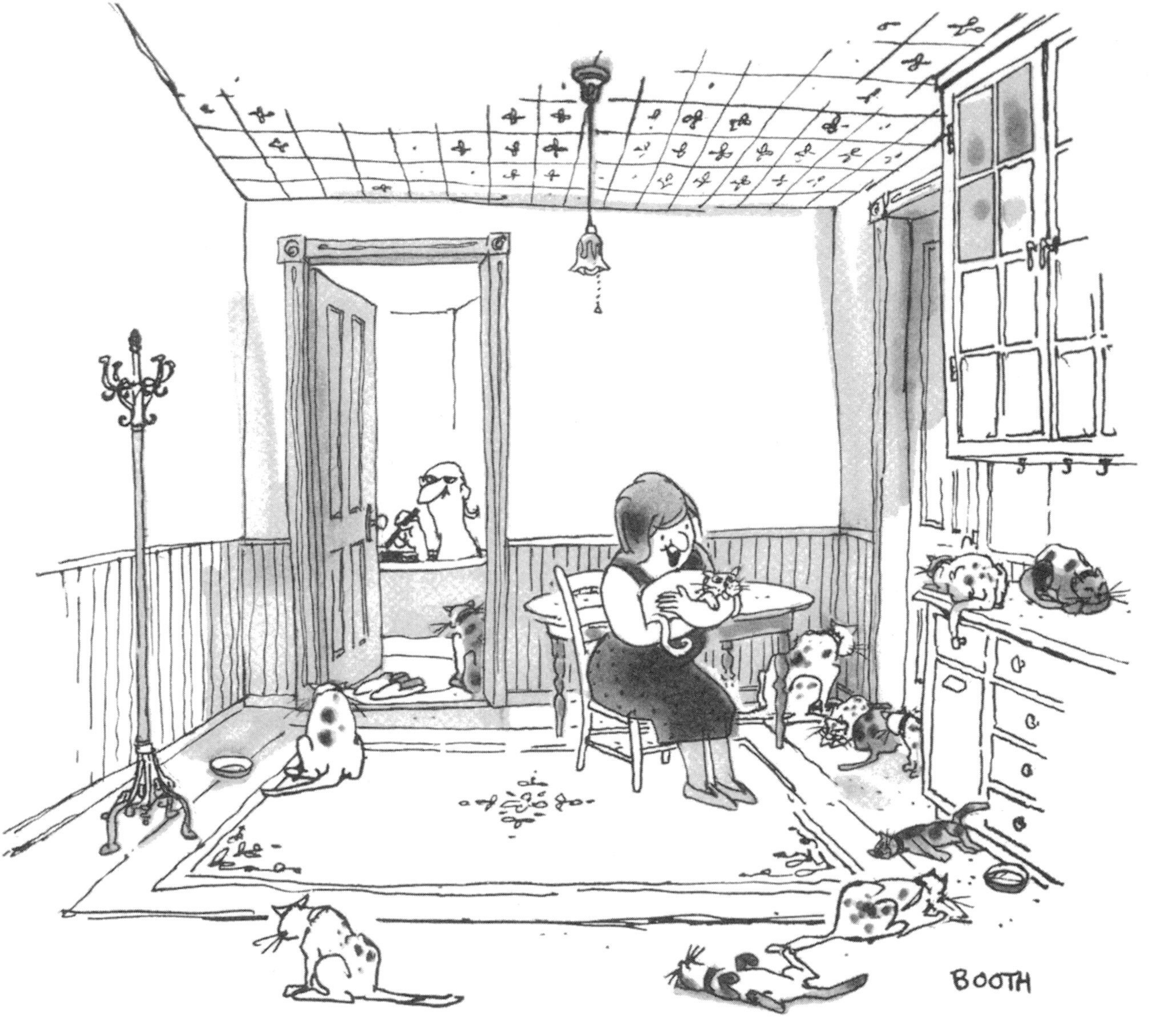
BOOTH

"Putty took a wife. Her name was Pussums, and she bore him Little Gentleman, Biddy Boo, Savor Tooth, Fluffy, Harry Cat, and Caesar. Then Little Gentleman begat Little Gentleman II and Friday and Twinkle Toes and Possum Tail and . . ."

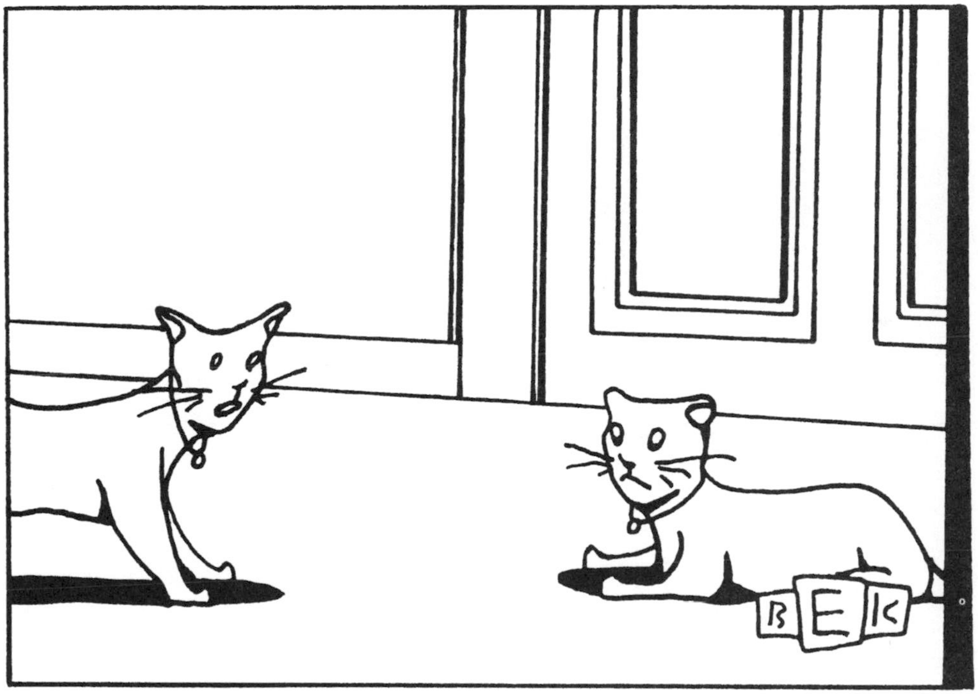
BEK

"People are O.K., but I prefer little pieces of string."

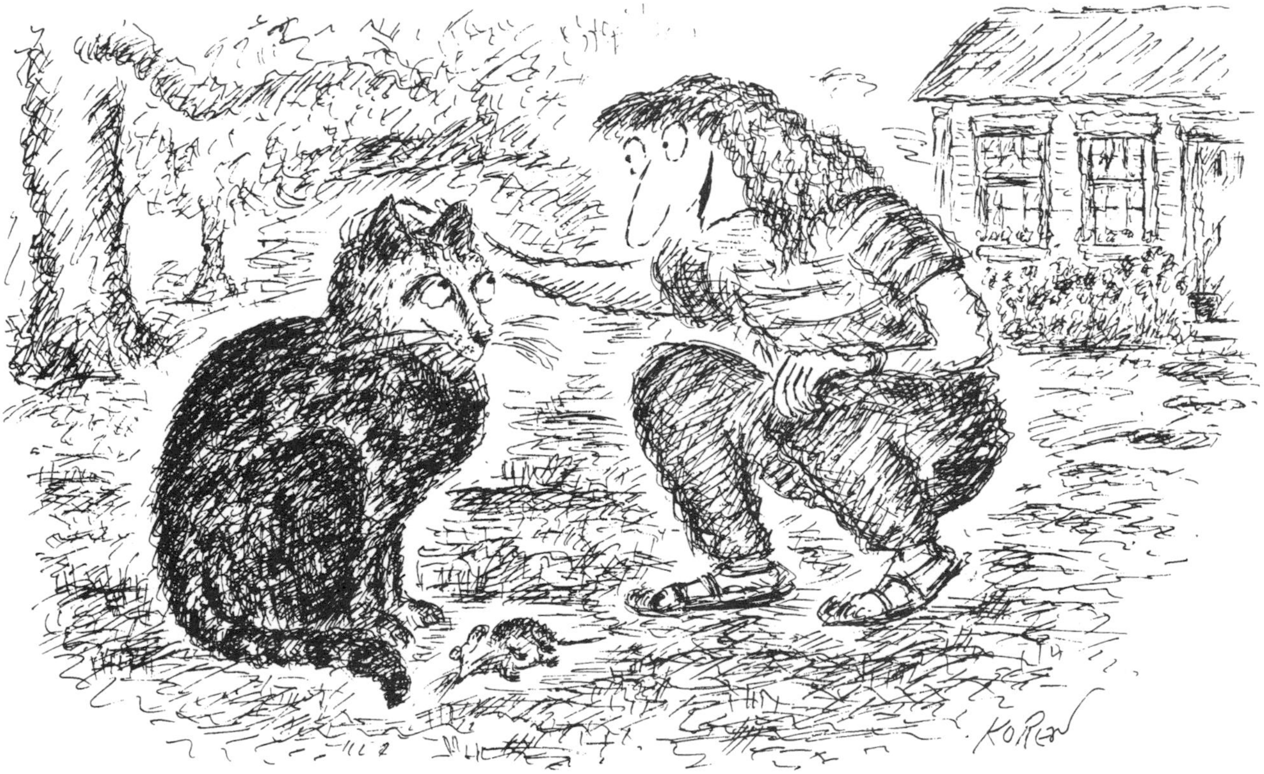
KOREN

"Do you ever miss New York?"

CHESHIRE CLASS REUNION

"Samantha is Harry's, but Homer here is mine from a
previous marriage."

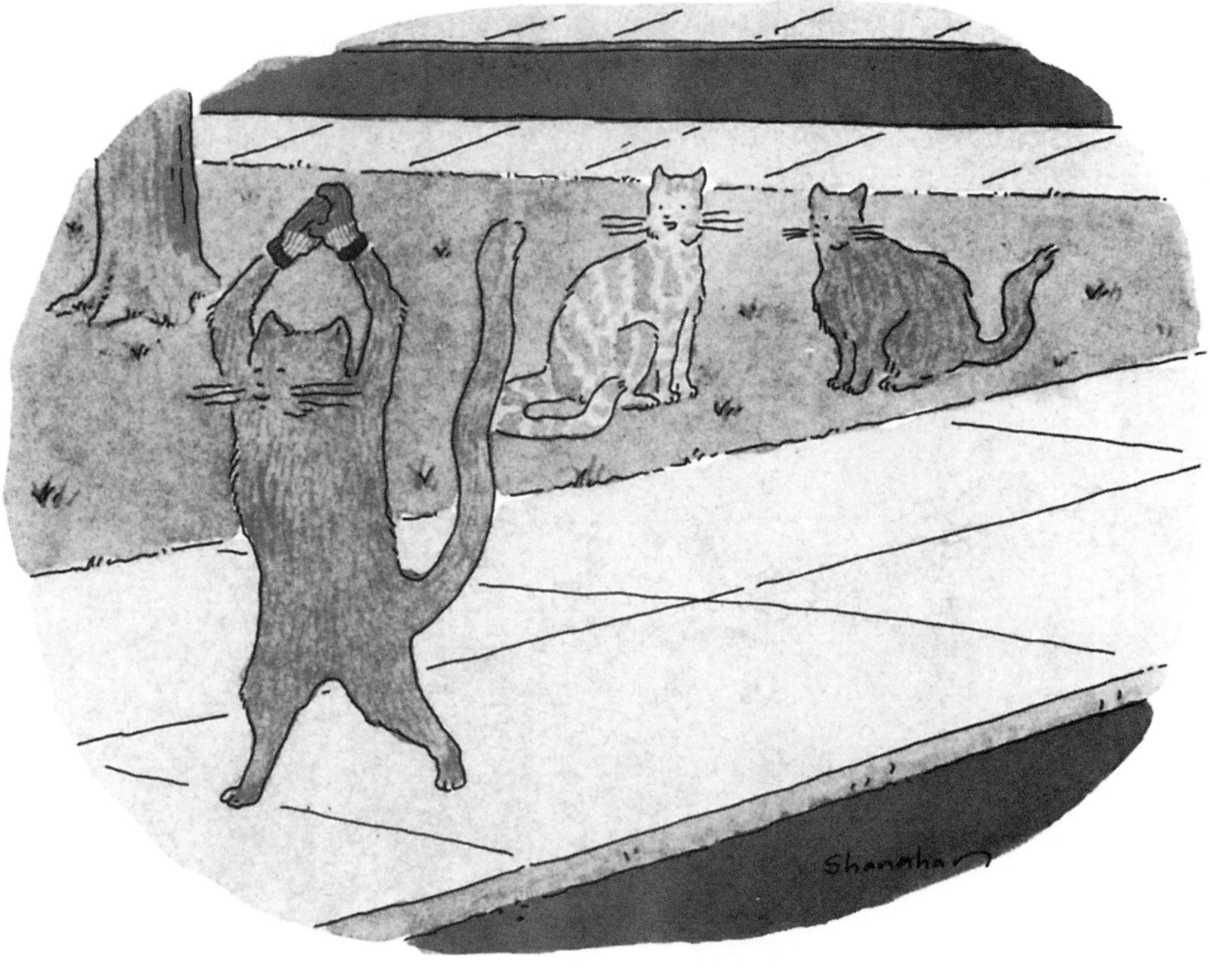
Shanahan

"He may have found his mittens, but he's lost all sense of propriety."

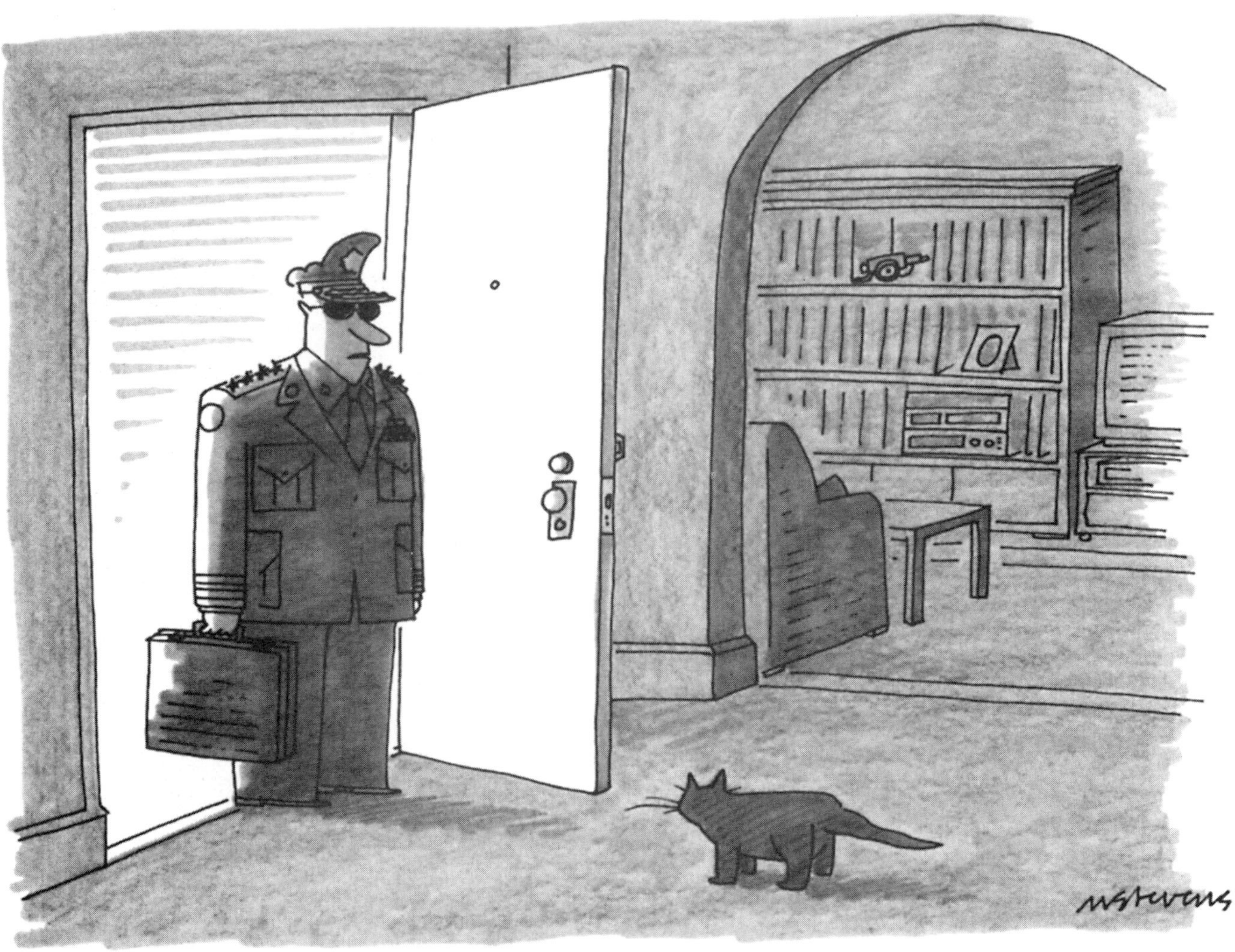

"As you were."

"Before Prozac, she loathed company."

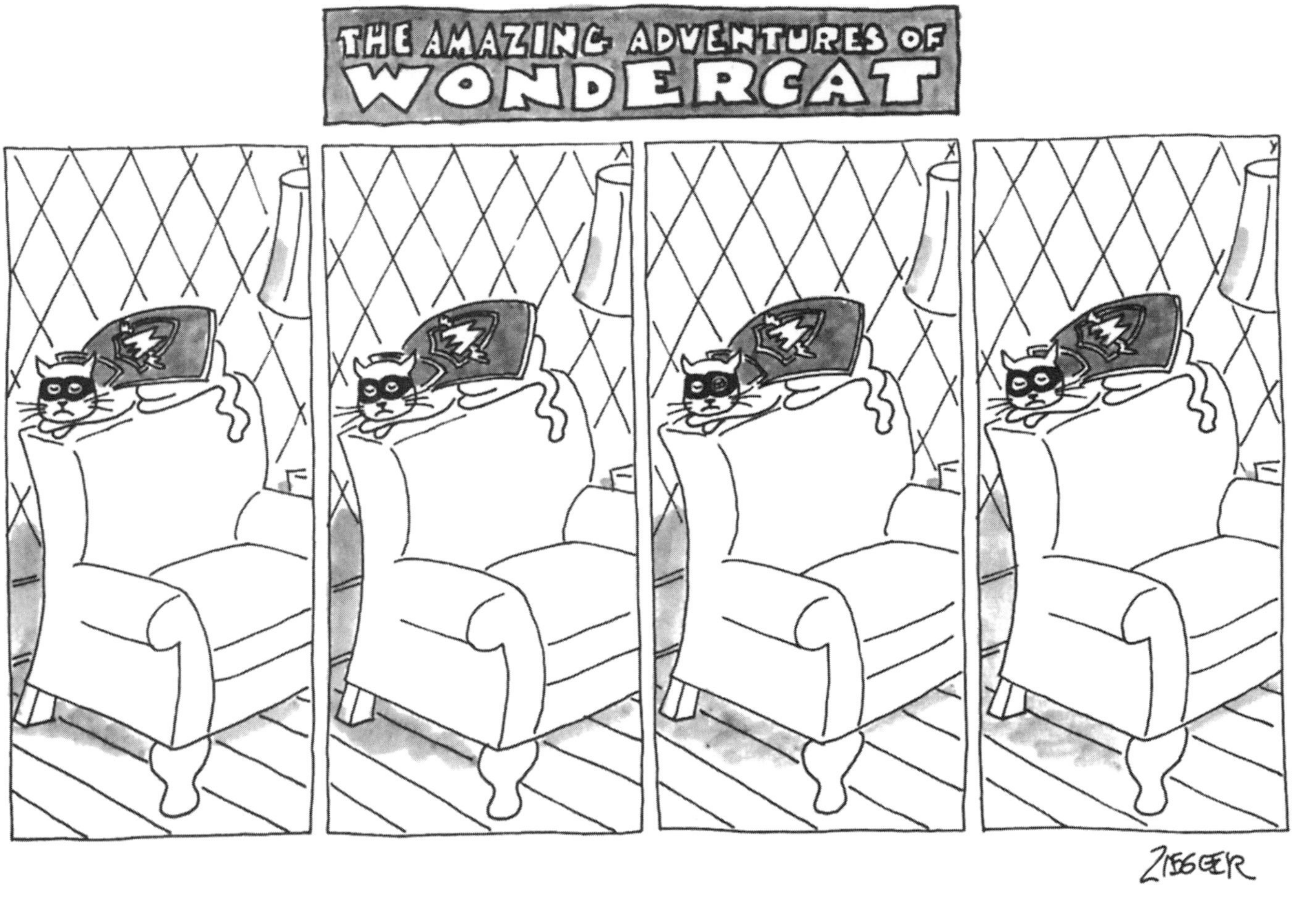
THE AMAZING ADVENTURES OF
WONDERCAT
ZIEGLER

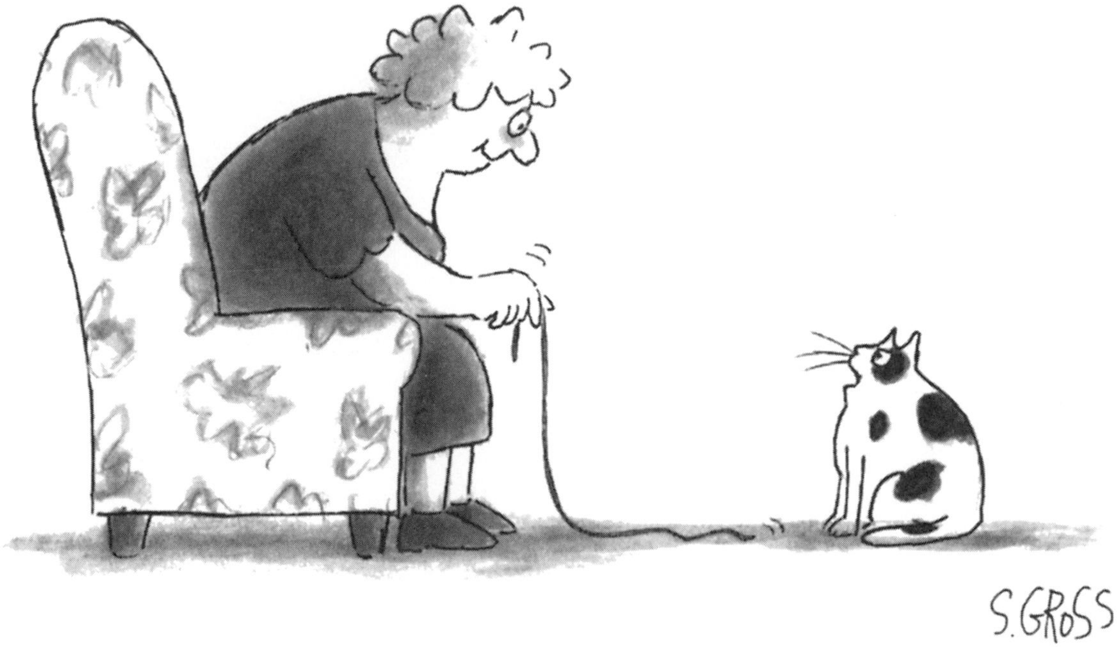
S.GROSS

"We are not amused."

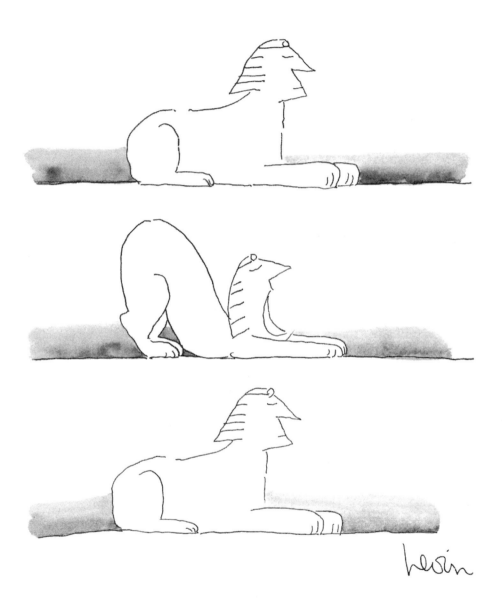

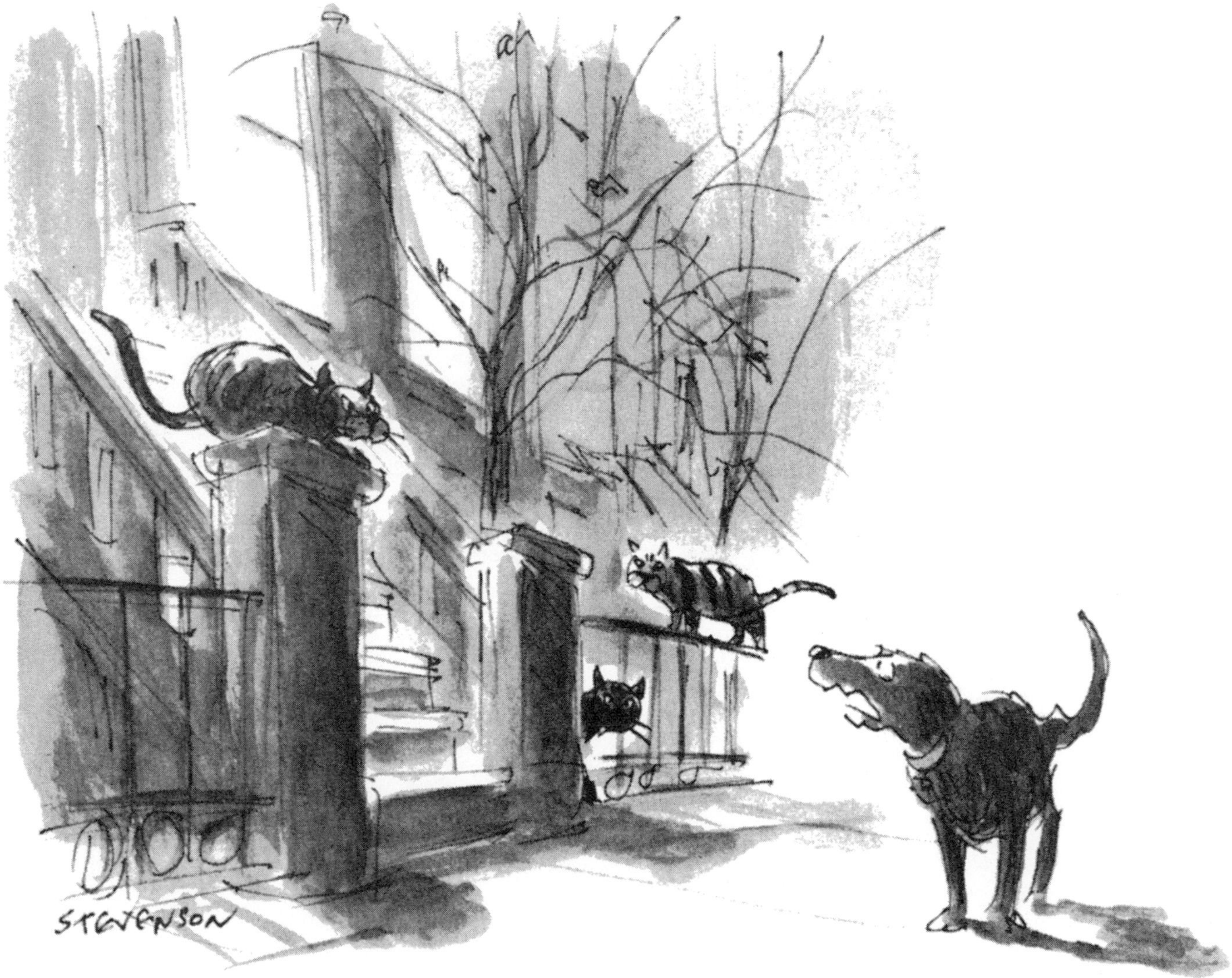
STEVENSON

"Big deal! You're still all bums to me."

THE CAT LADY

Anthony

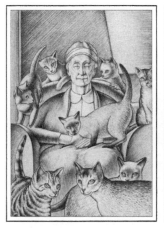

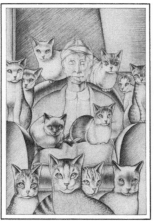

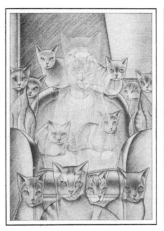

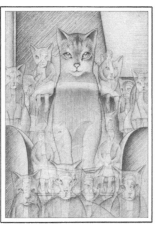

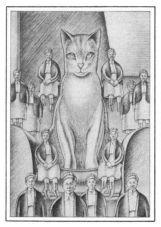

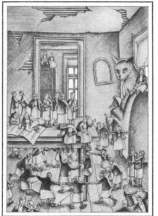

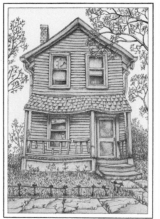

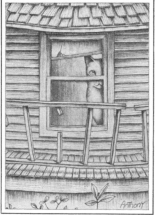

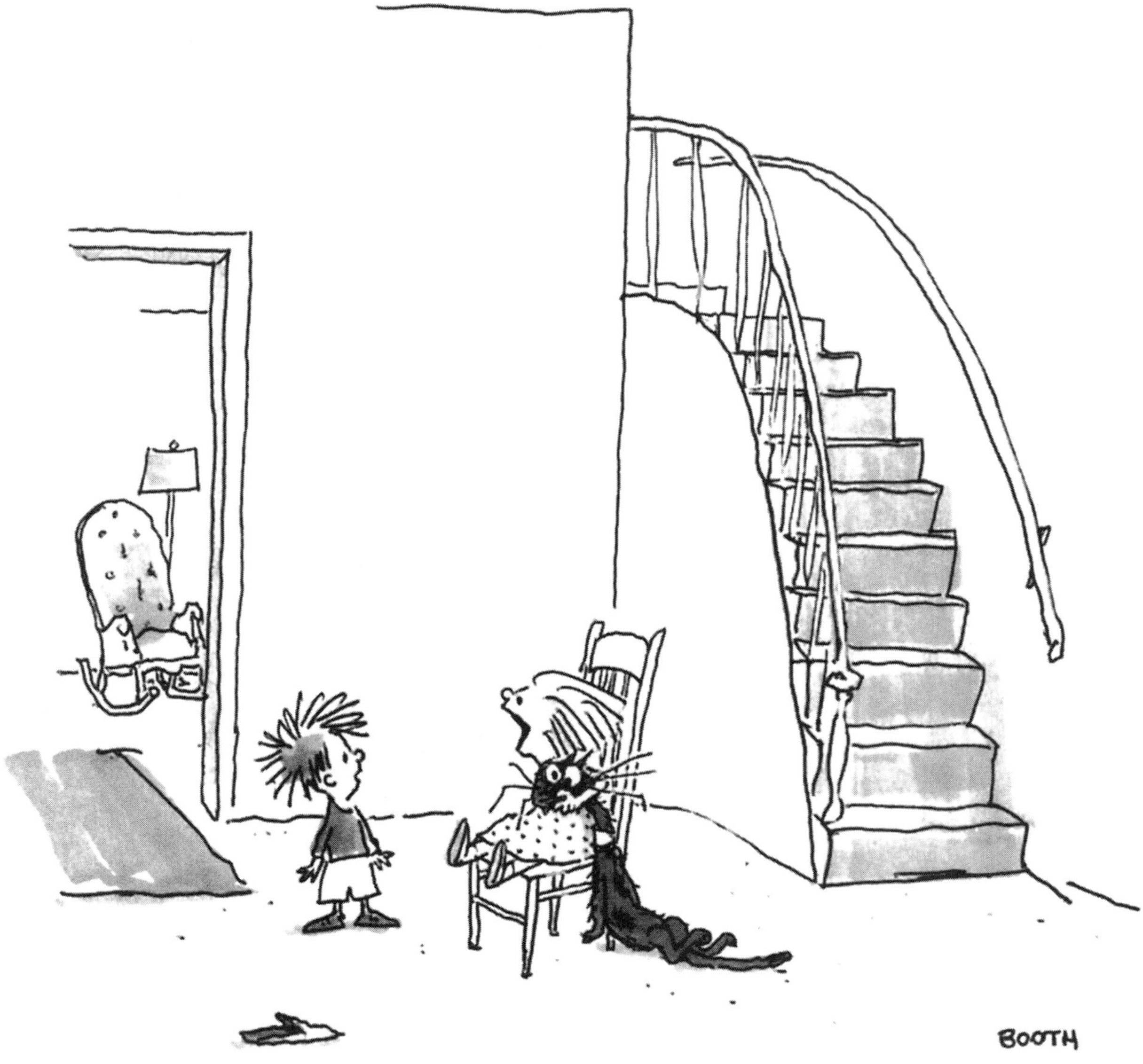
BOOTH

"All you really need in life is the love of a good cat."

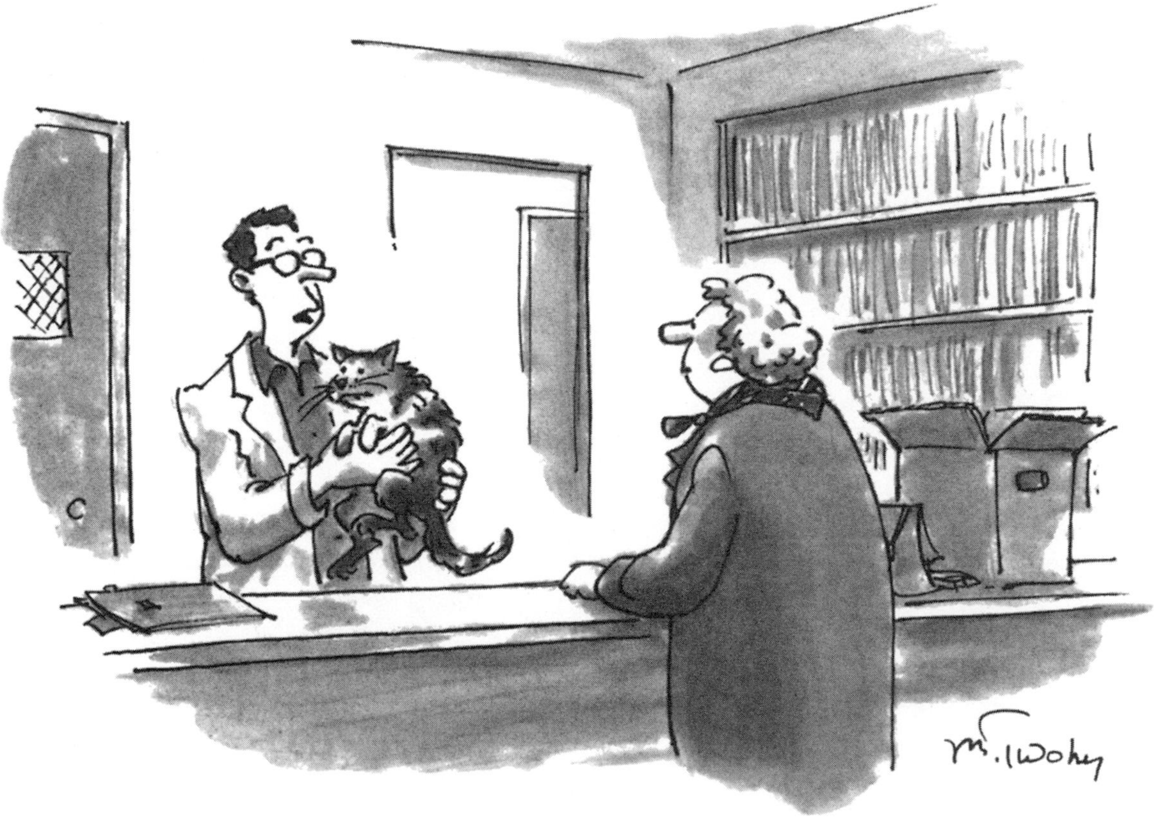
M. Twohy

"I'm afraid we'll have to keep him overnight. Are you going to need a loaner?"

WHO'S REALLY RUNNING THE CITY

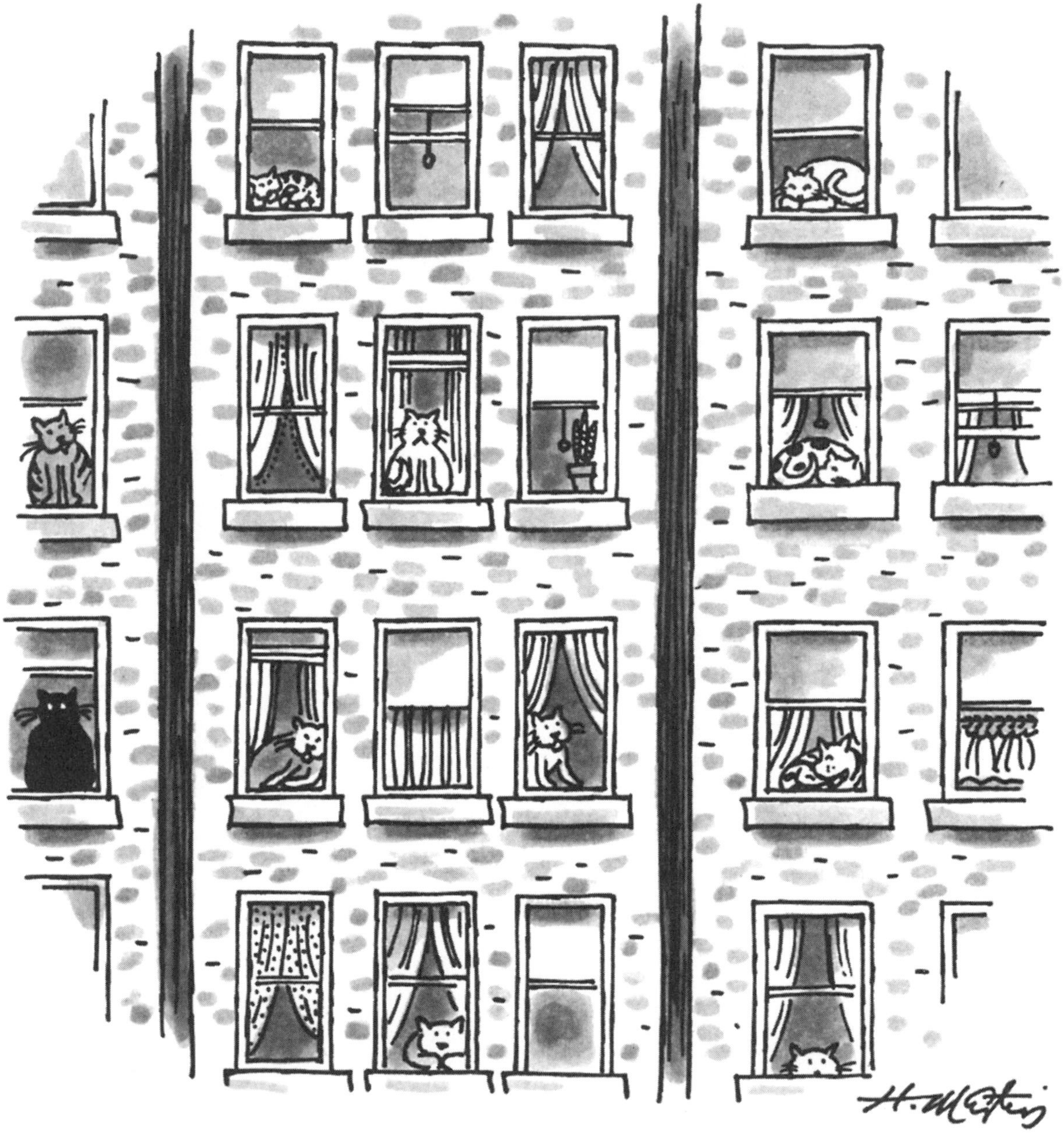

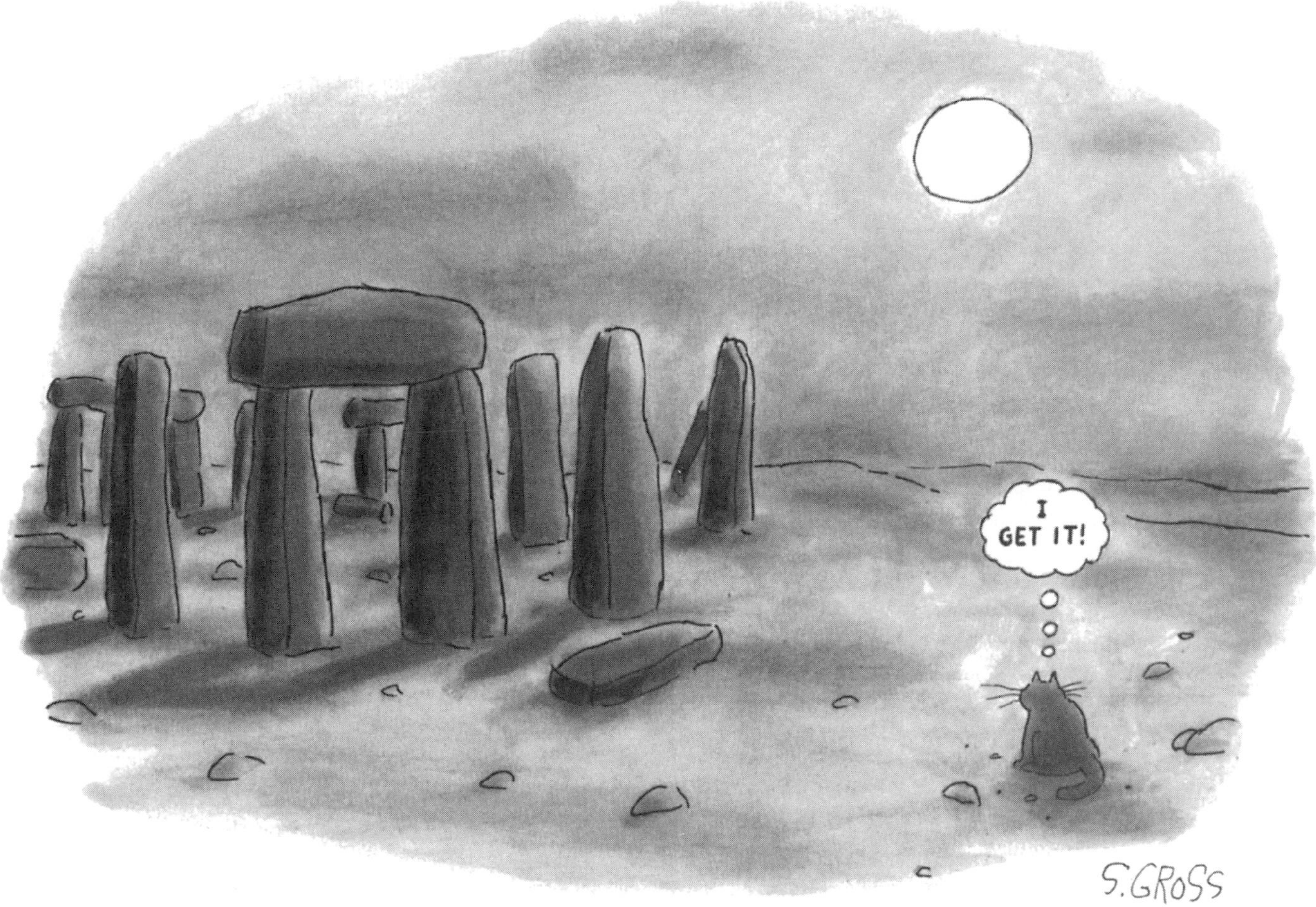
I GET IT!
S. GROSS

A LATE ENTRY FOR "POOR RICHARD'S ALMANACK"

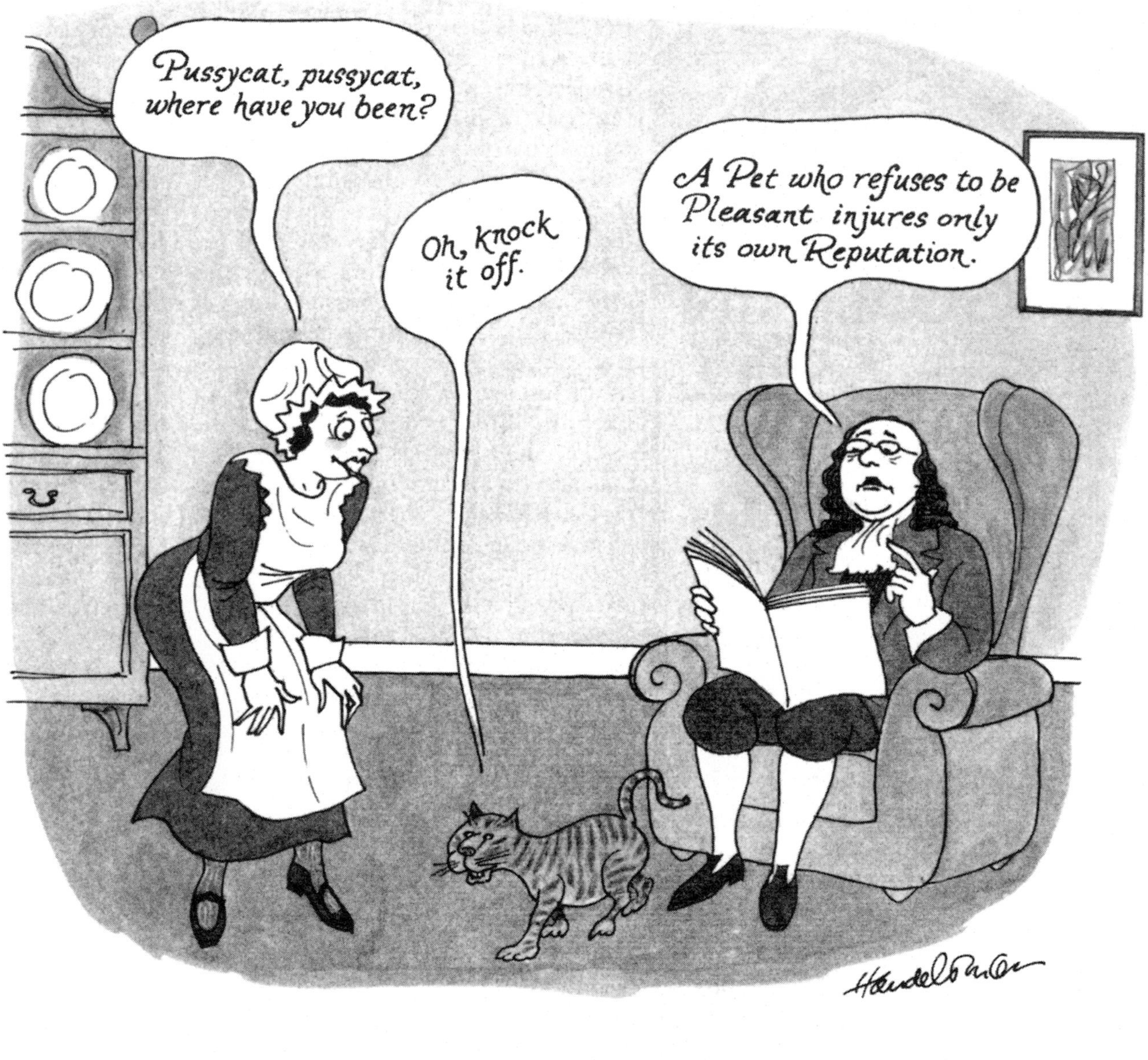
Pussycat, pussycat, where have you been?
Oh, knock it off.
A Pet who refuses to be Pleasant injures only its own Reputation.

"The phrase you're groping for is "Thank you.""

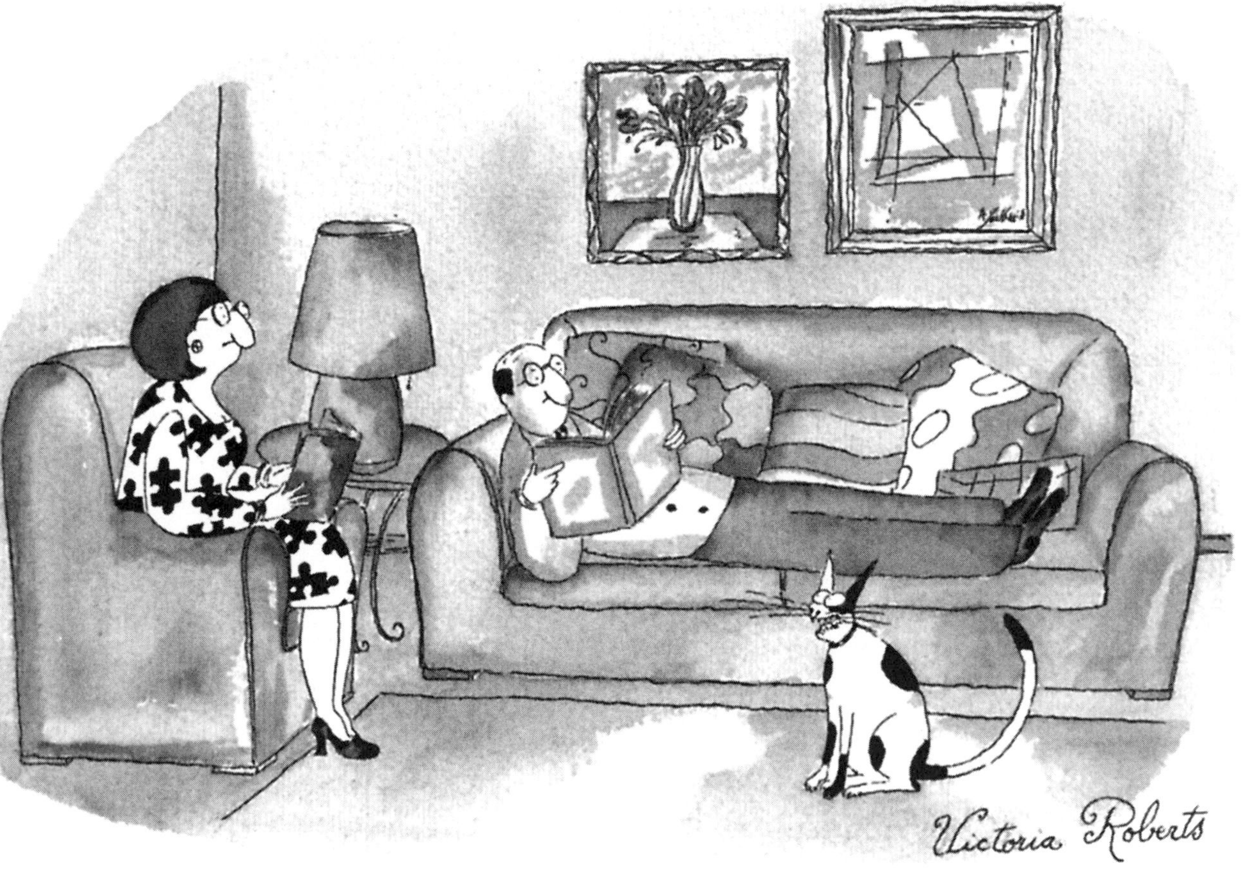
Victoria Roberts

"I need some answers, people."

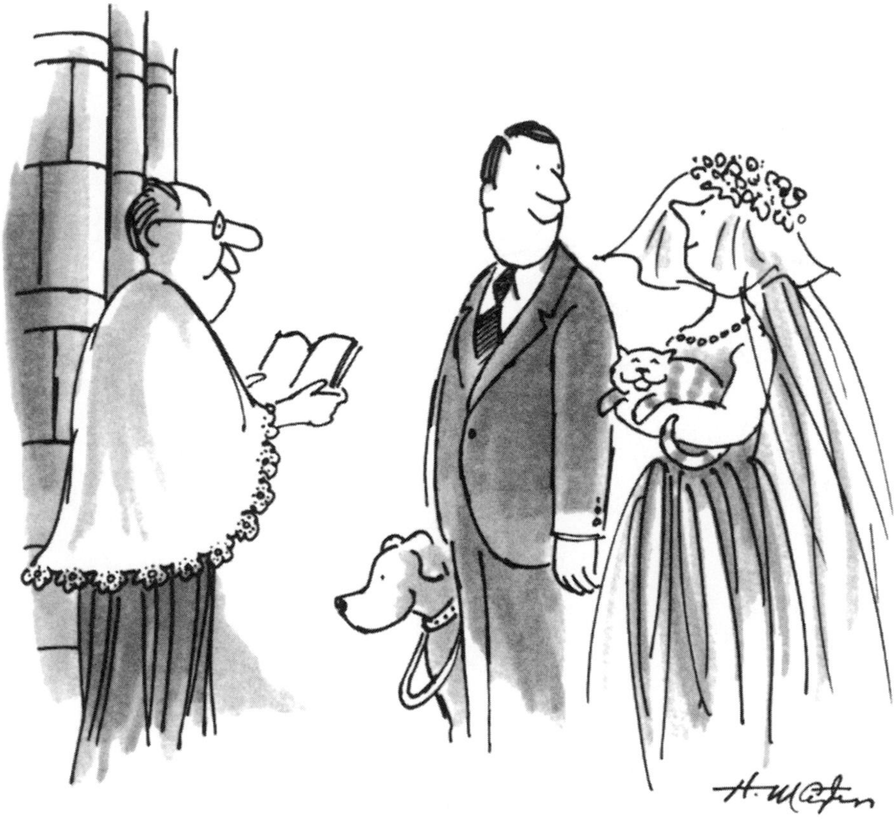
H. Martin

"Do you, Edward and King, take Susan and Fluffy, to have and to hold . . ."

"*Mom always liked you and Pinkie and Spike and
Custard and Fluffy best.*"

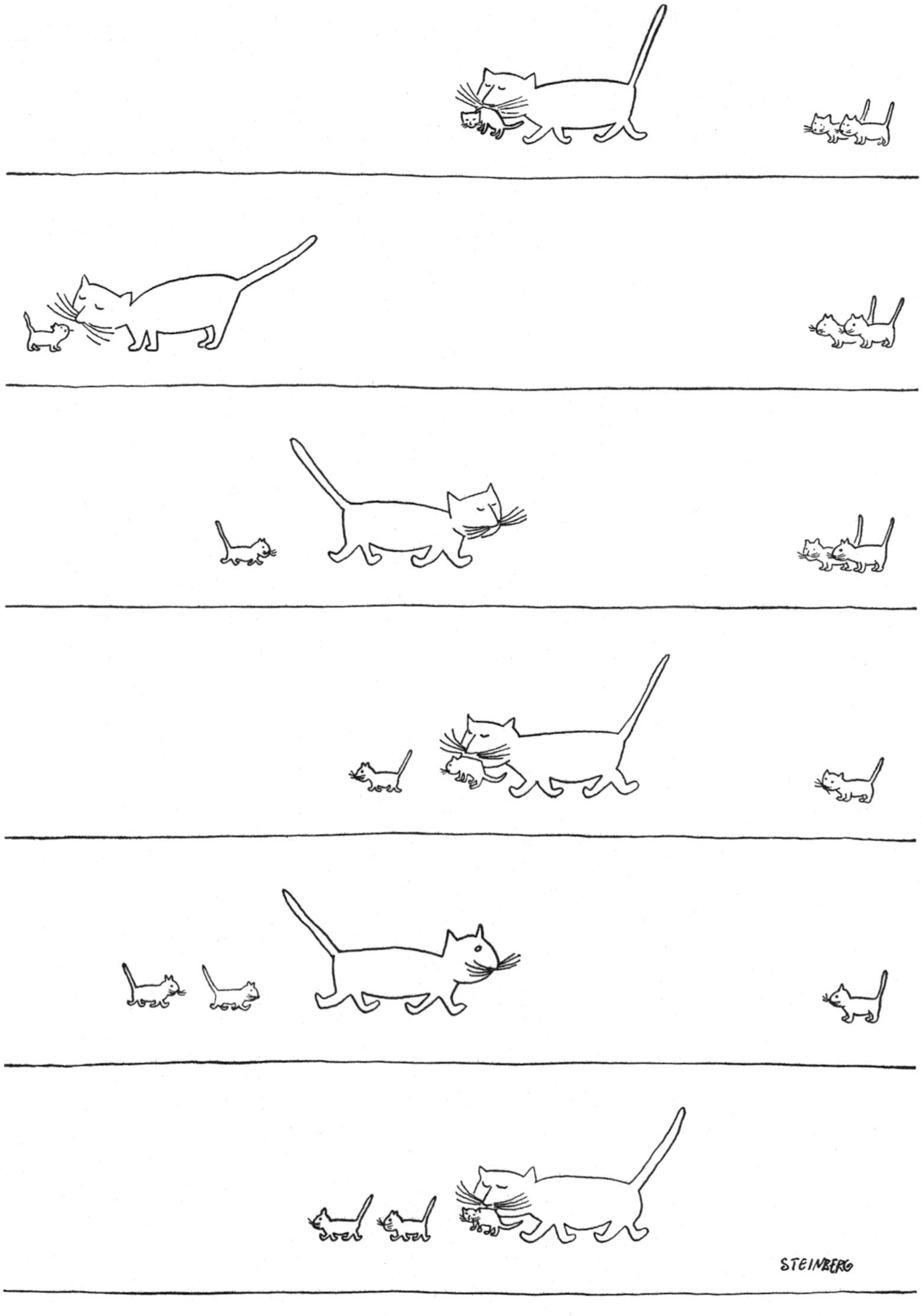
STEINBERG

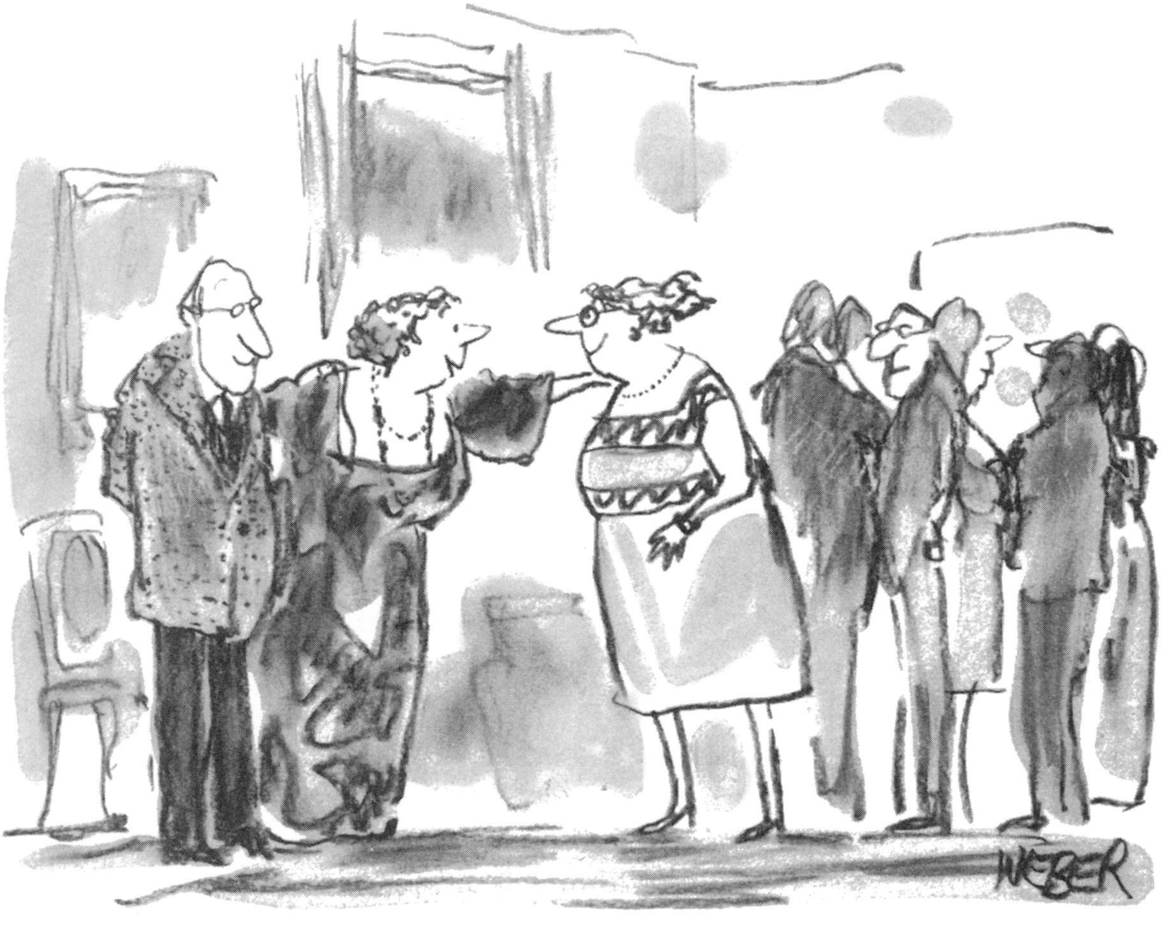
WEBER

"Dolly—Gregory Strong, author of 'A World History of Cats.' Need I say more?"

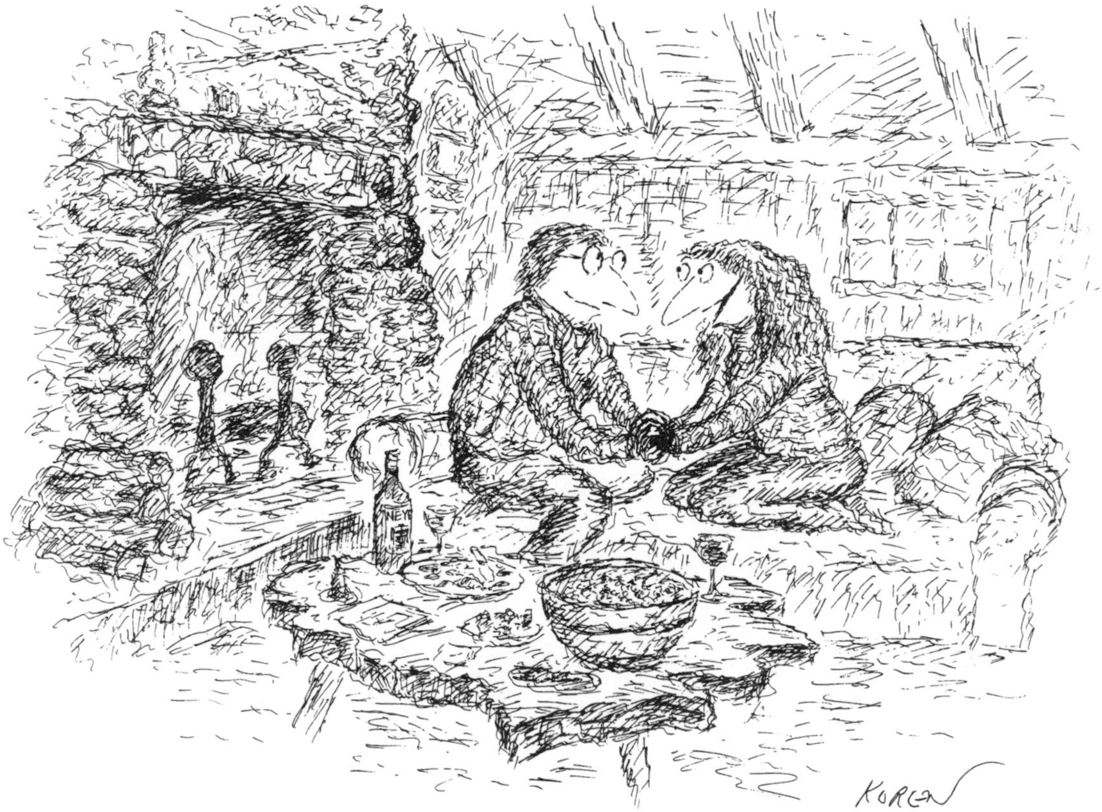
KOREN

"Honey, I don't want to hide anything from you. I collect pictures of cats in my spare time."

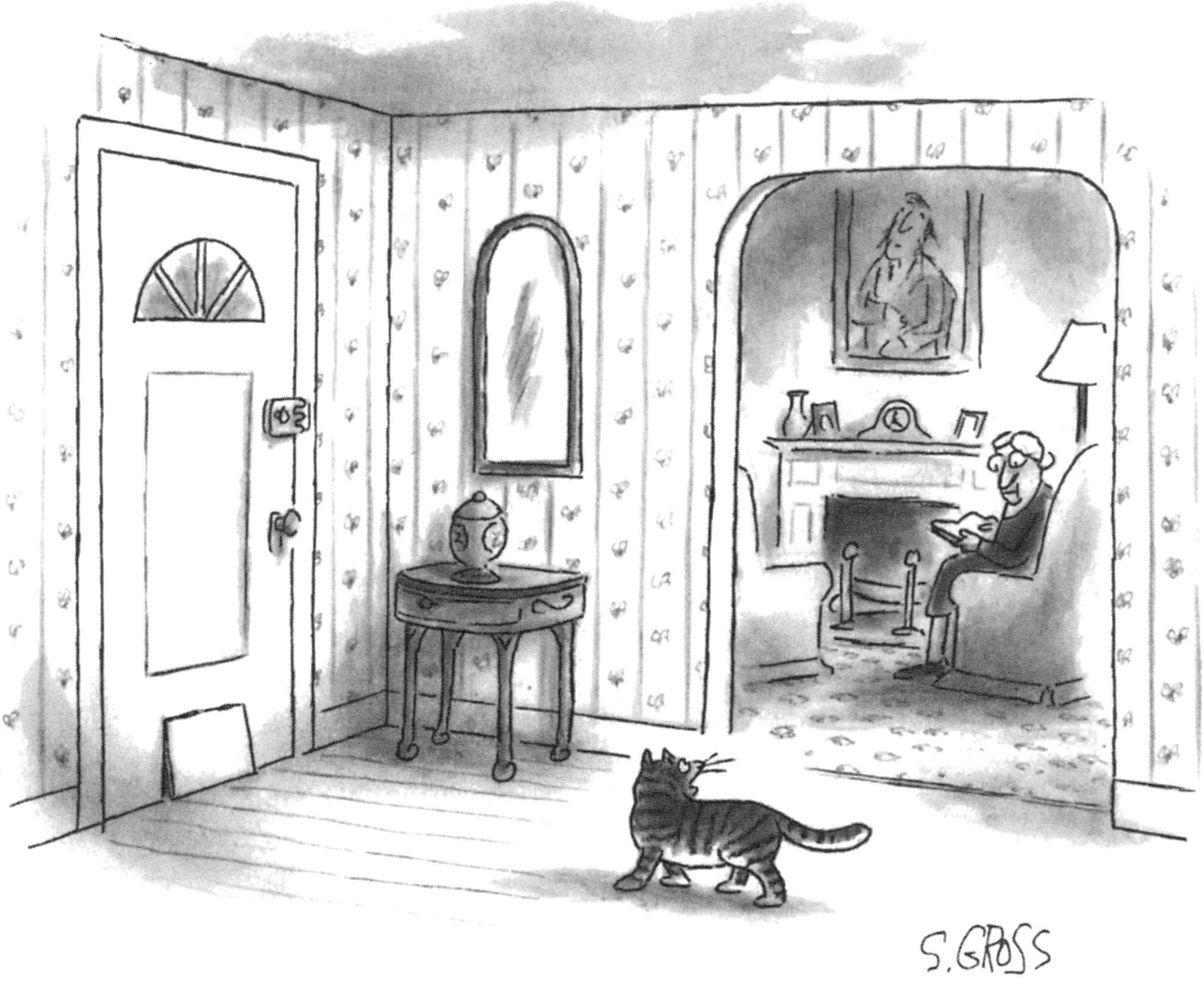
S. GROSS

"I'm going out. Do you need any voles?"

"She's not all over you, but she gets the job done."

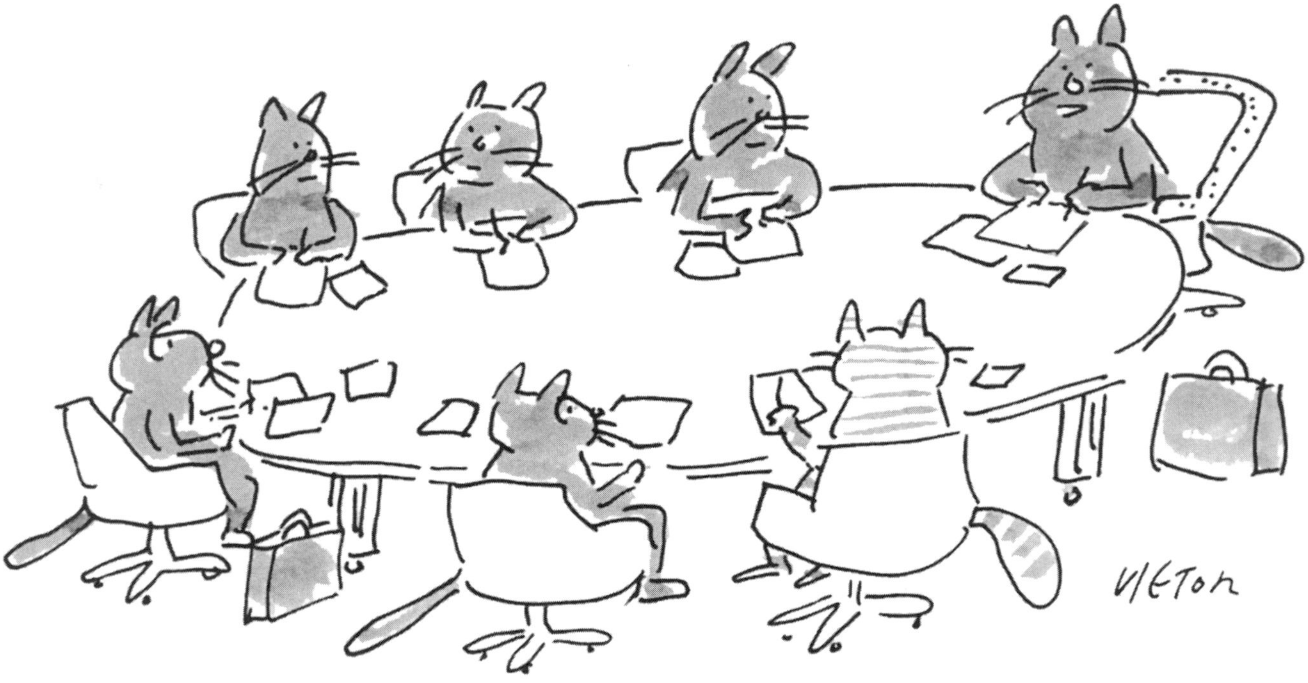
VIETOR

"O.K., just for our records, how many of you have been getting away with sleeping on top of the VCR?"

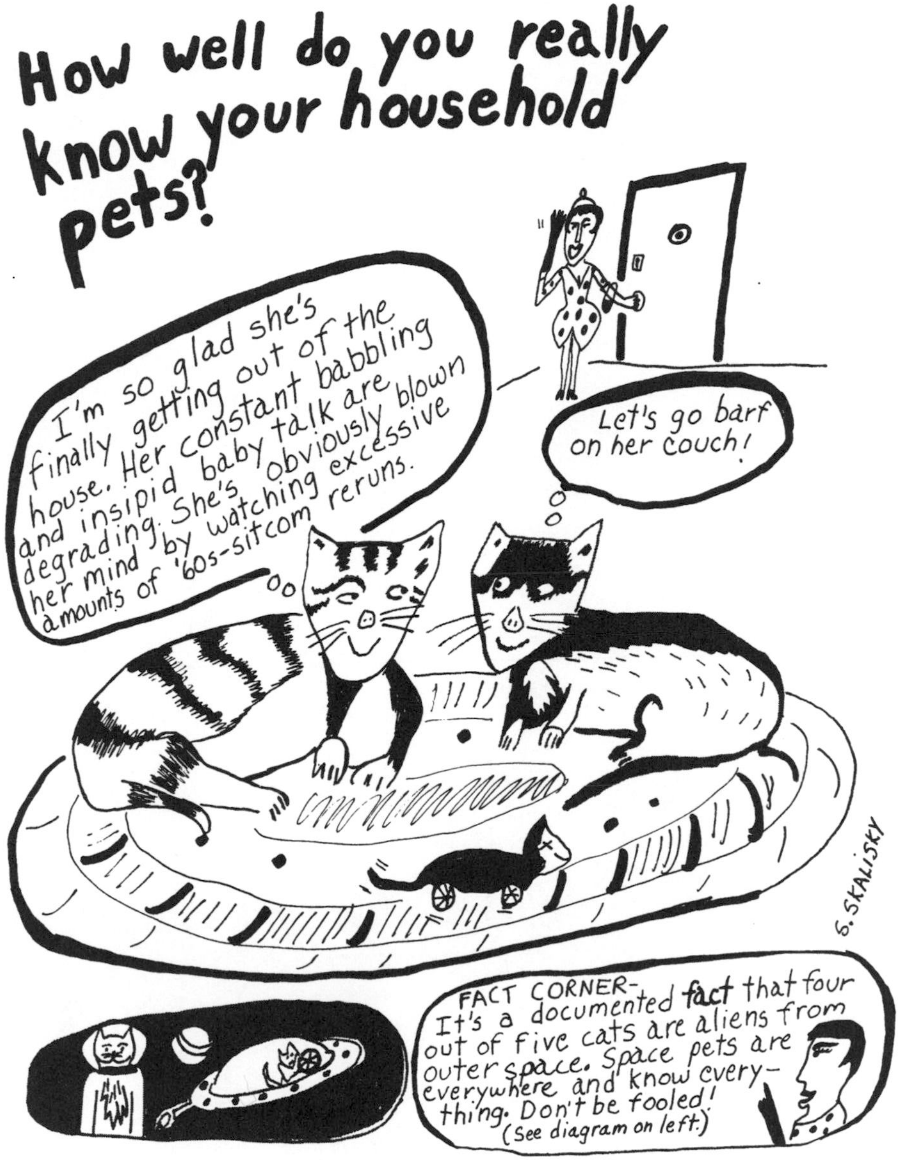
How well do you really know your household pets?
I'm so glad she's finally getting out of the house. Her constant babbling and insipid baby talk are degrading. She's obviously blown her mind by watching excessive amounts of '60s-sitcom reruns.
Let's go barf on her couch!
G. SKALISKY
FACT CORNER- It's a documented fact that four out of five cats are aliens from outer space. Space pets are everywhere and know everything. Don't be fooled! (See diagram on left.)

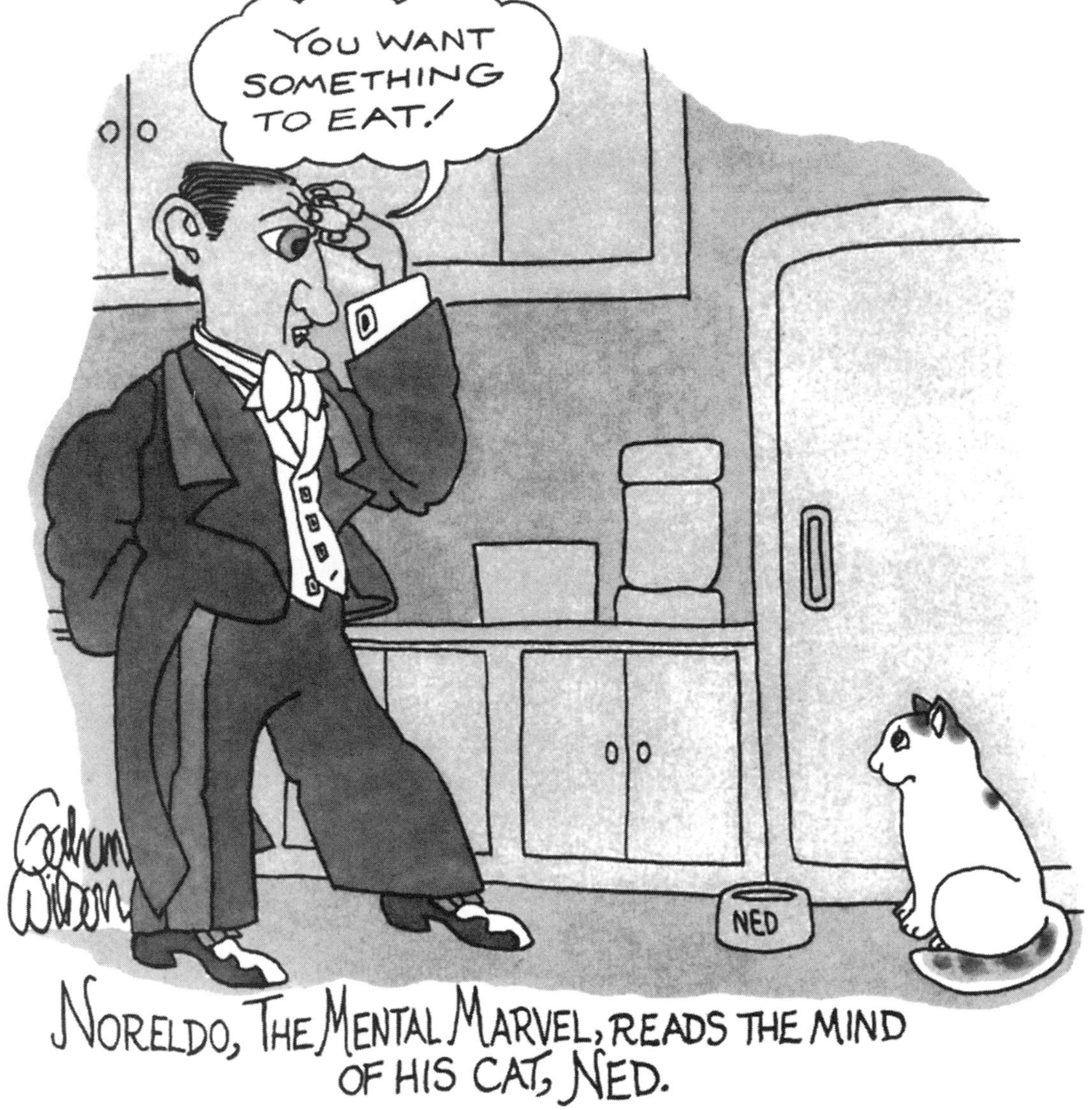
YOU WANT SOMETHING TO EAT!
NED

NORELDO, THE MENTAL MARVEL, READS THE MIND OF HIS CAT, NED.

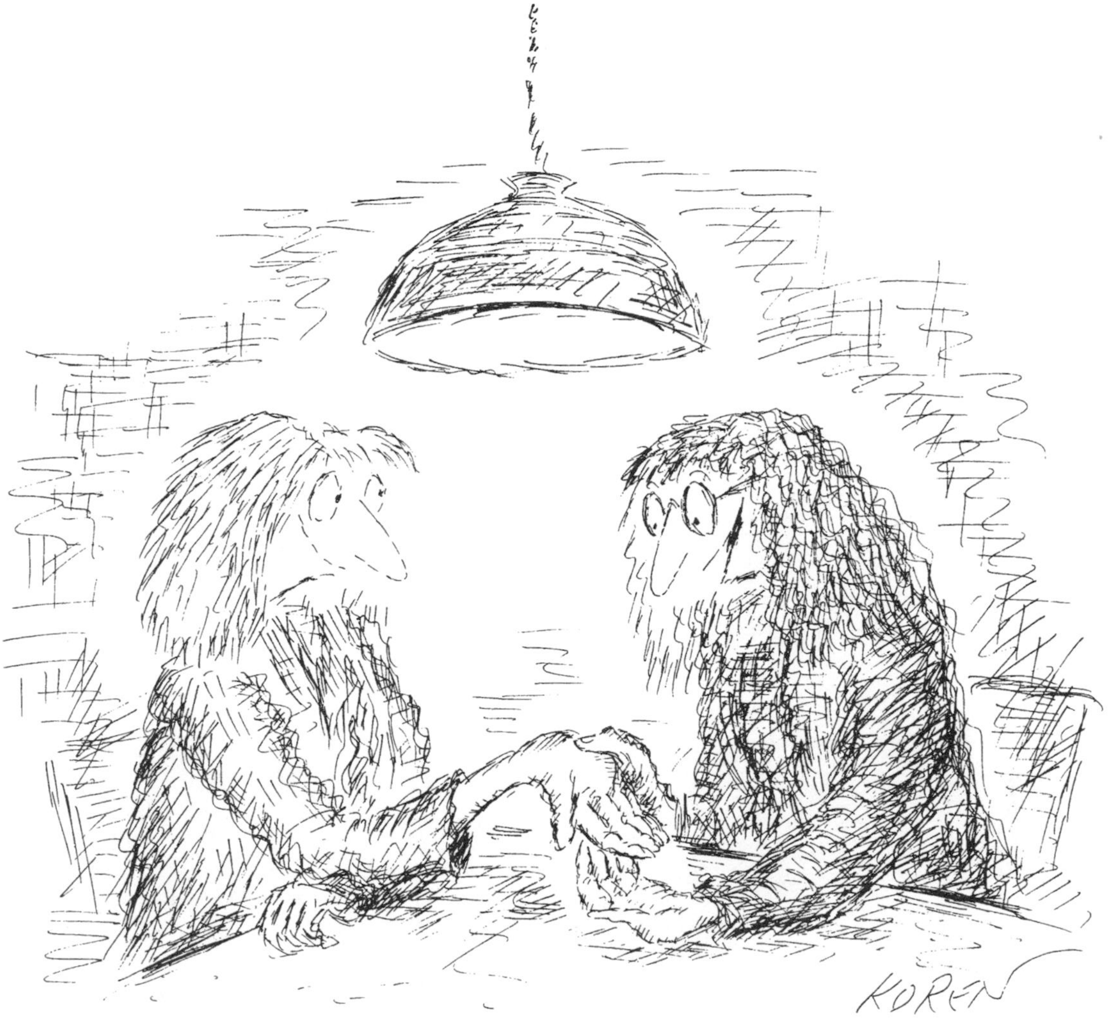
KOREN

"A wonderful cat is coming into your life."

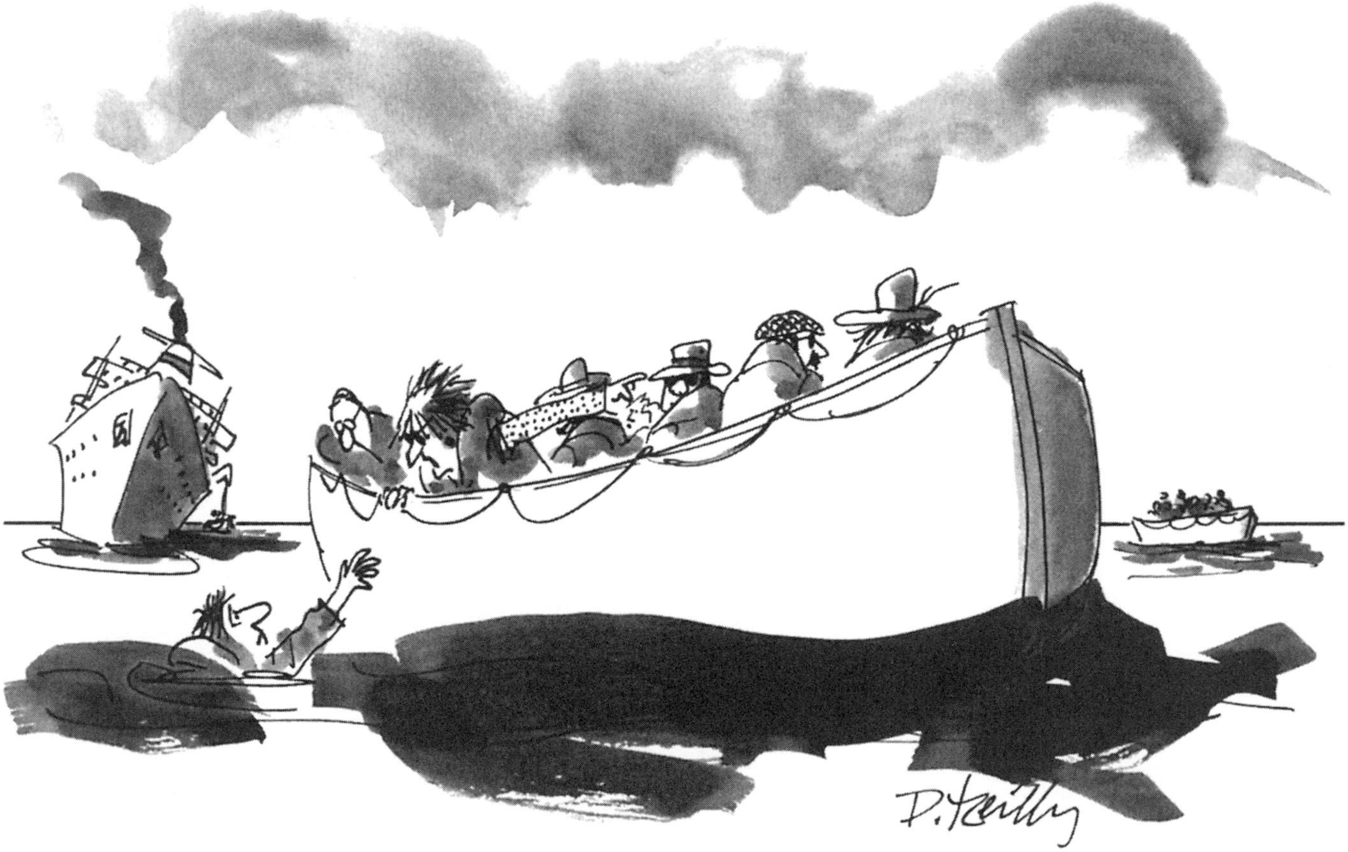
D. Reilly

"Sorry, we're all cat people. The dog people are in that boat over there."

"Oh, lots of things were different when I was a child. For one thing,
it wasn't all cats. It was dogs."

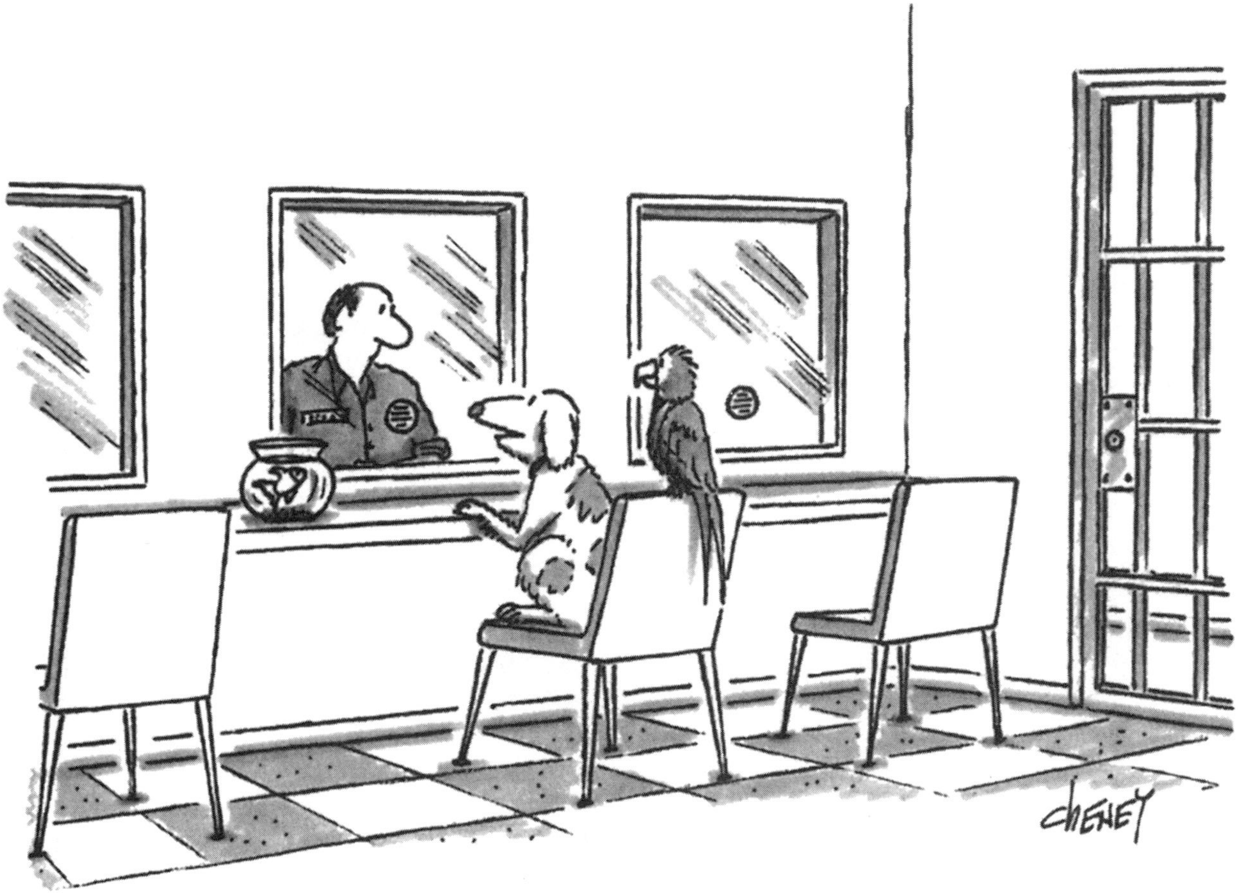
CHENEY

"We tried to talk her into coming, but you know how cats are."

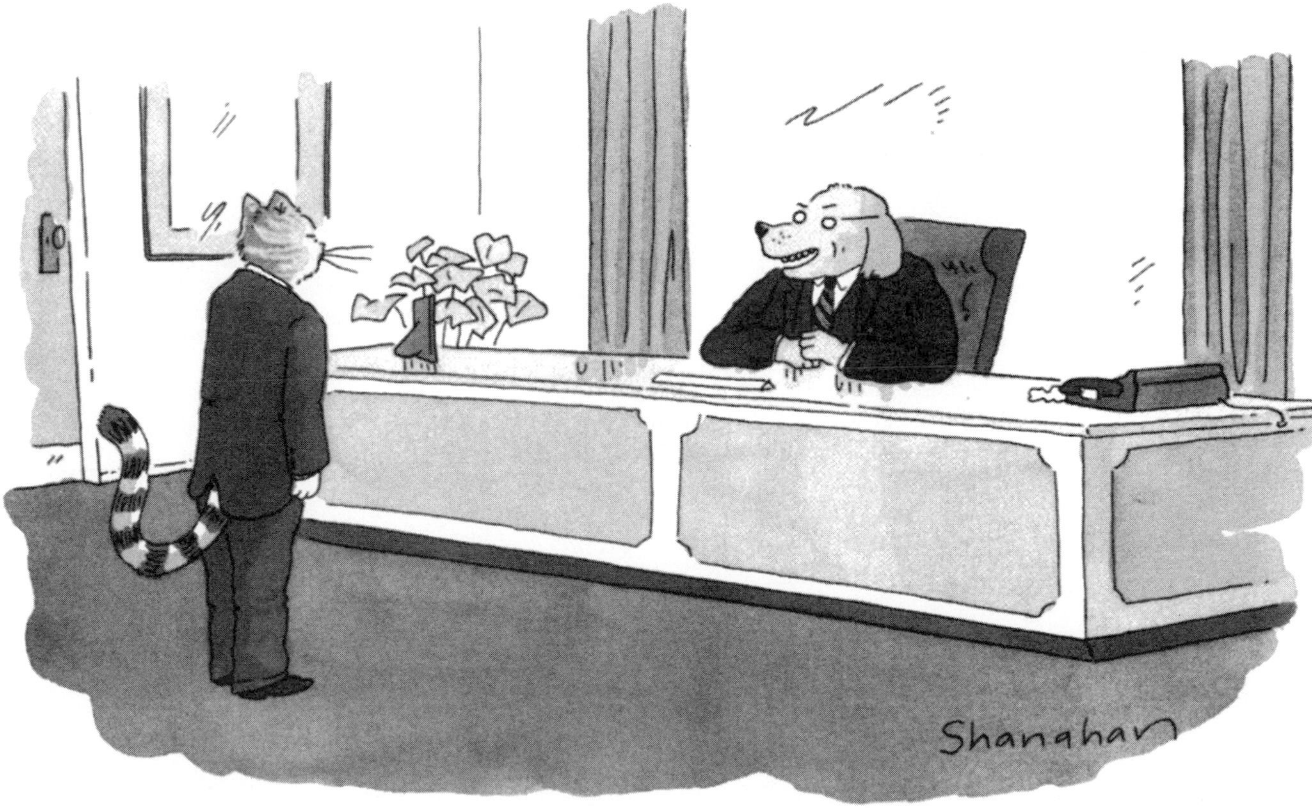
Shanahan

"I'm not worried about you, Henley. You'll land on your feet."

1.

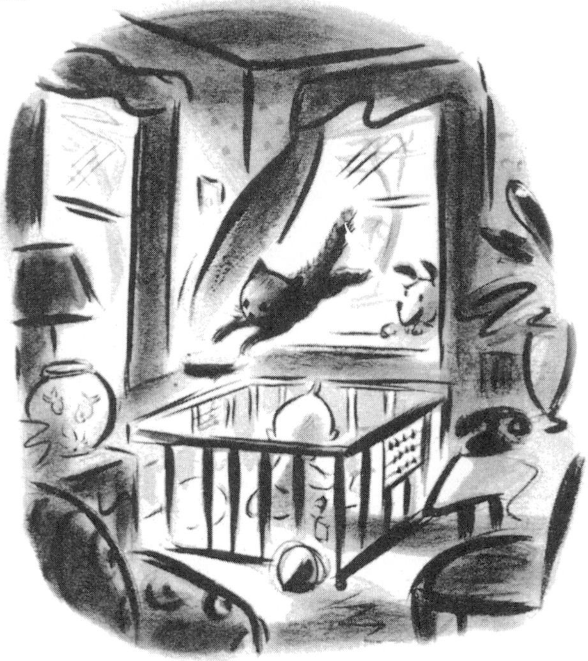

2.

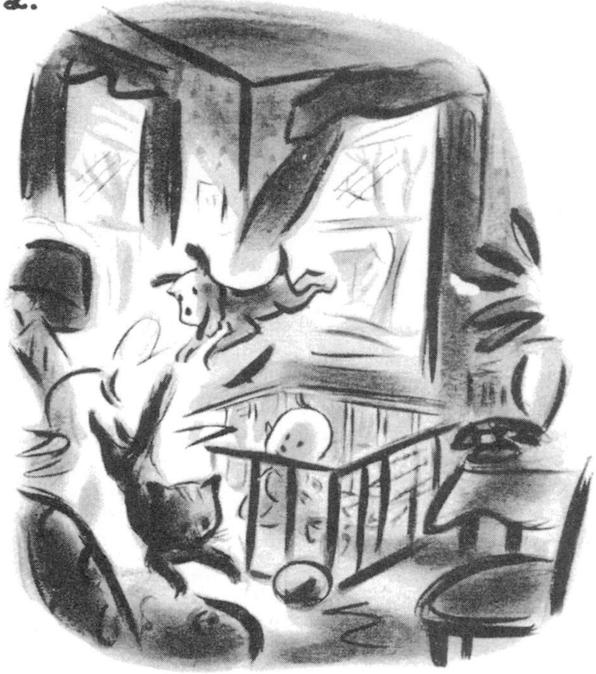

5.

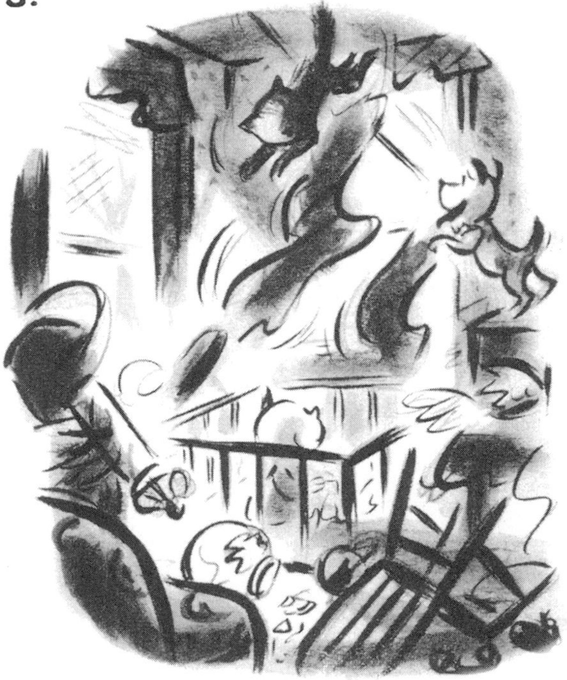

6.

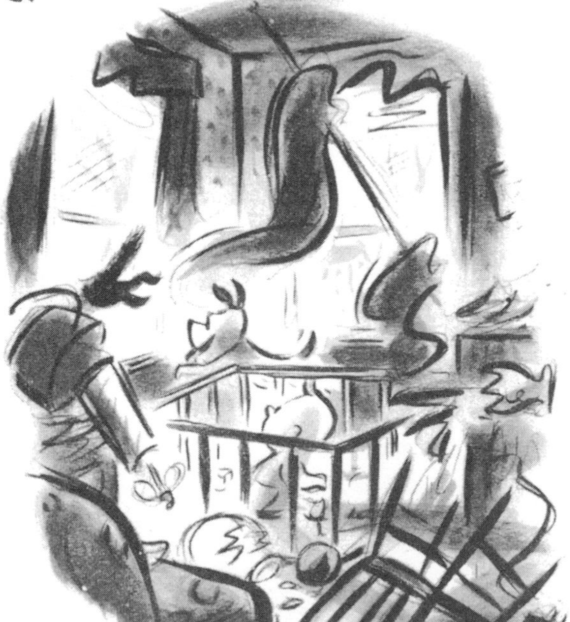

3.

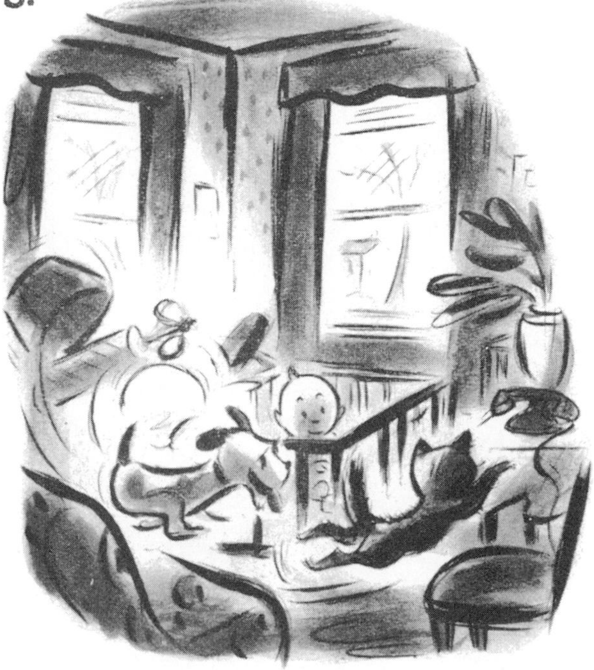

4.

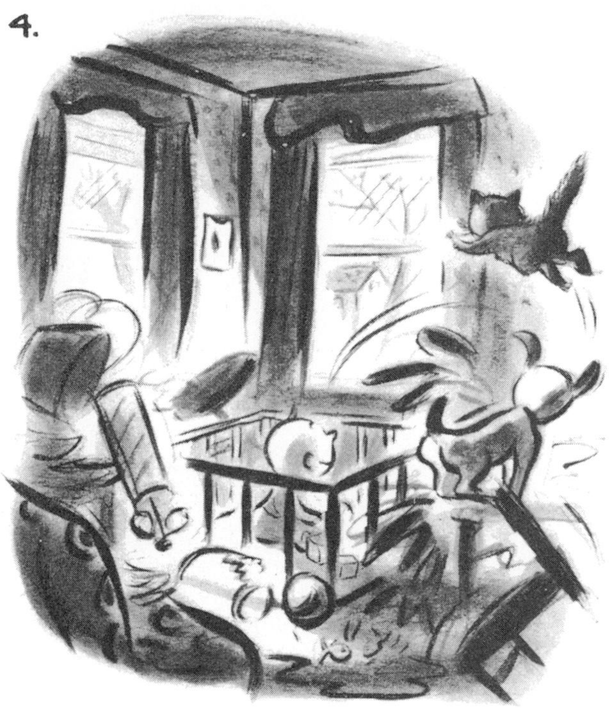

7.

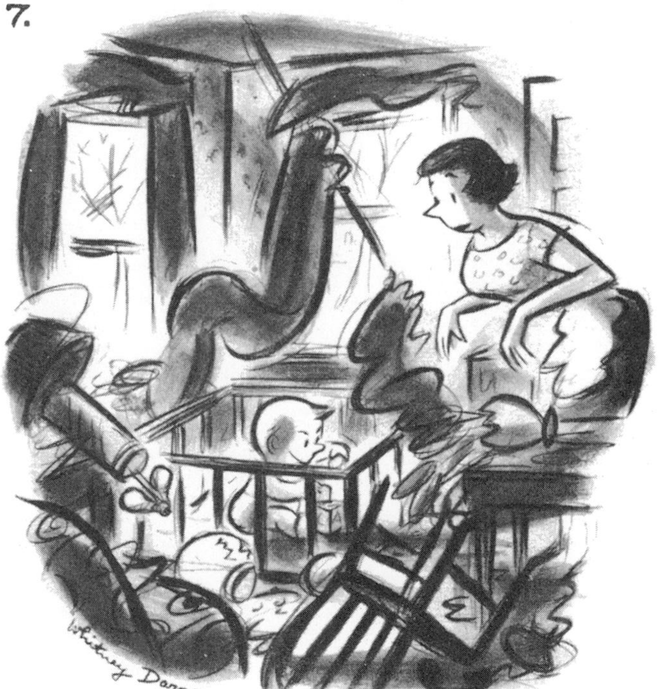
Whitney Darrow, Jr.

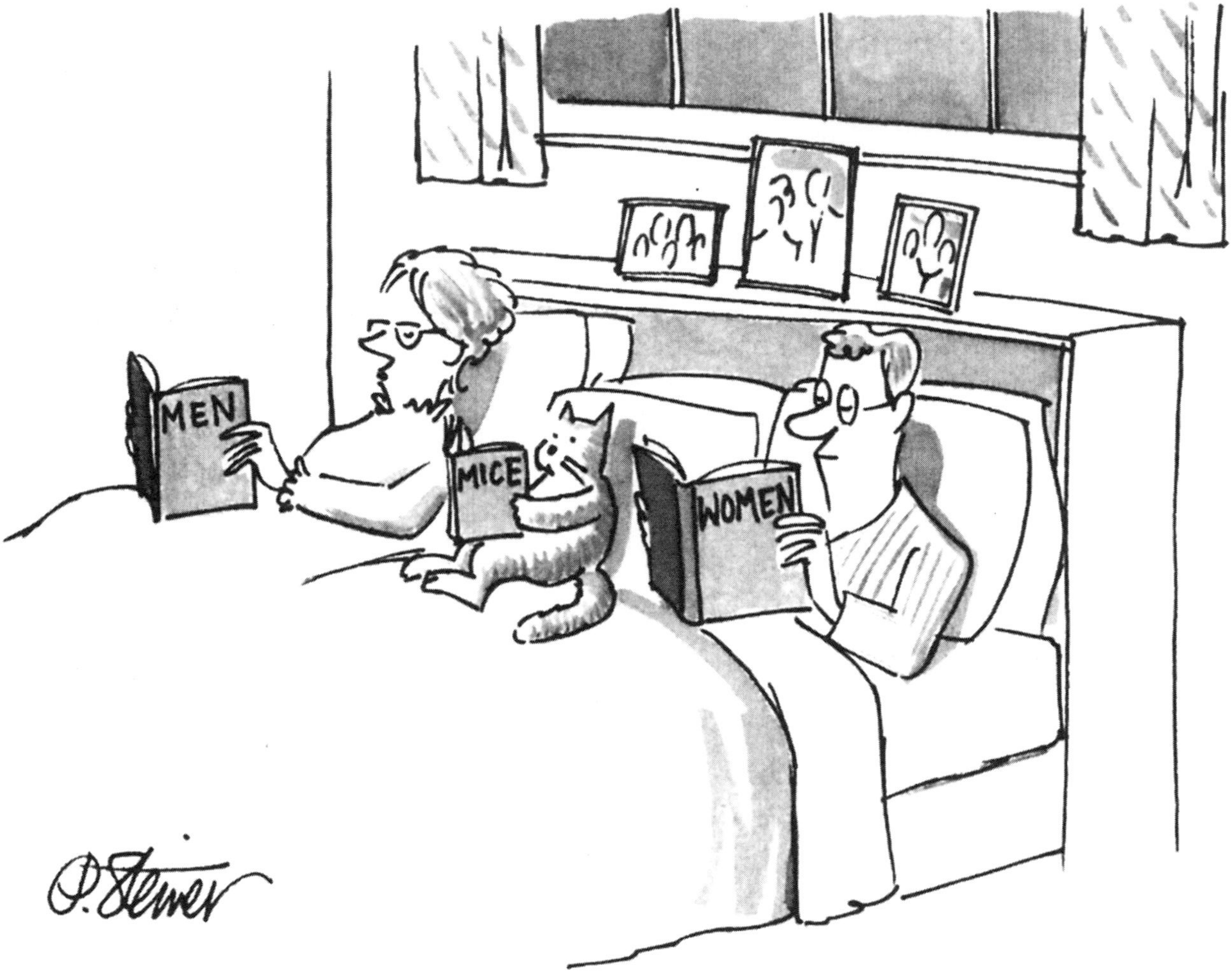
MEN
MICE
WOMEN
P. Steiner

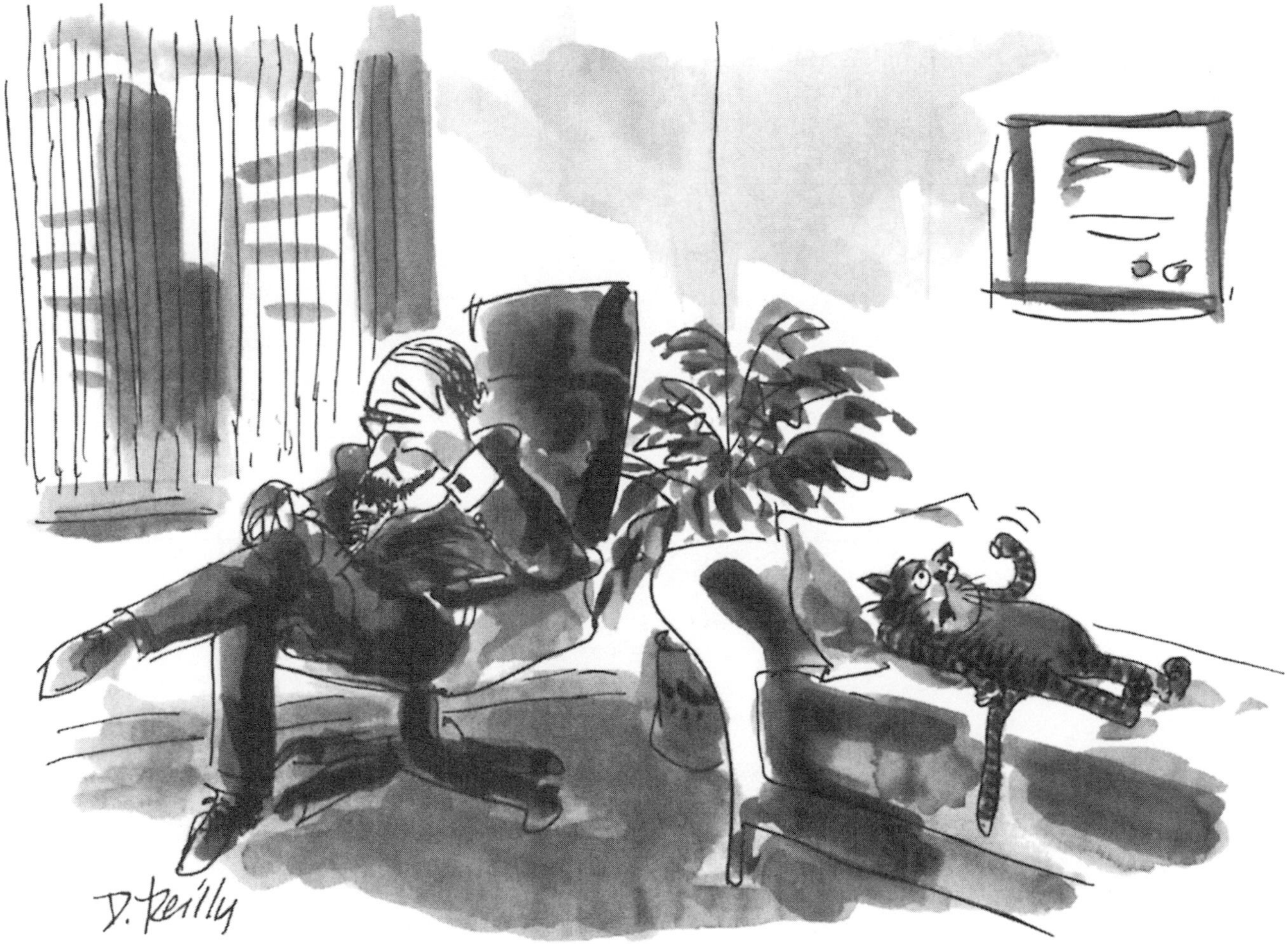
D. Reilly

"To this day, I can hear my mother's voice—harsh, accusing. 'Lost your mittens? You naughty kittens! Then you shall have no pie!'"

"Oh yeah? When's the last time you dragged anything in?"

"*I have a couple of other projects I'm excited about.*"

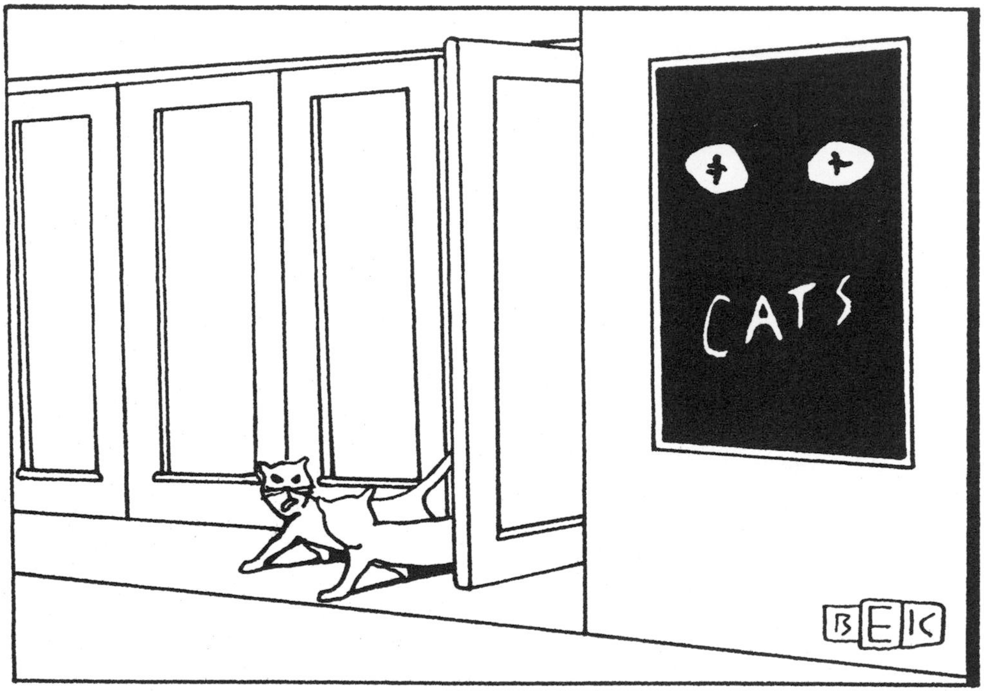
CATS
BEK

"It was so depressing. When I go to the theatre, I want to be entertained."

STAR

 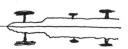

RATS

STEINBERG

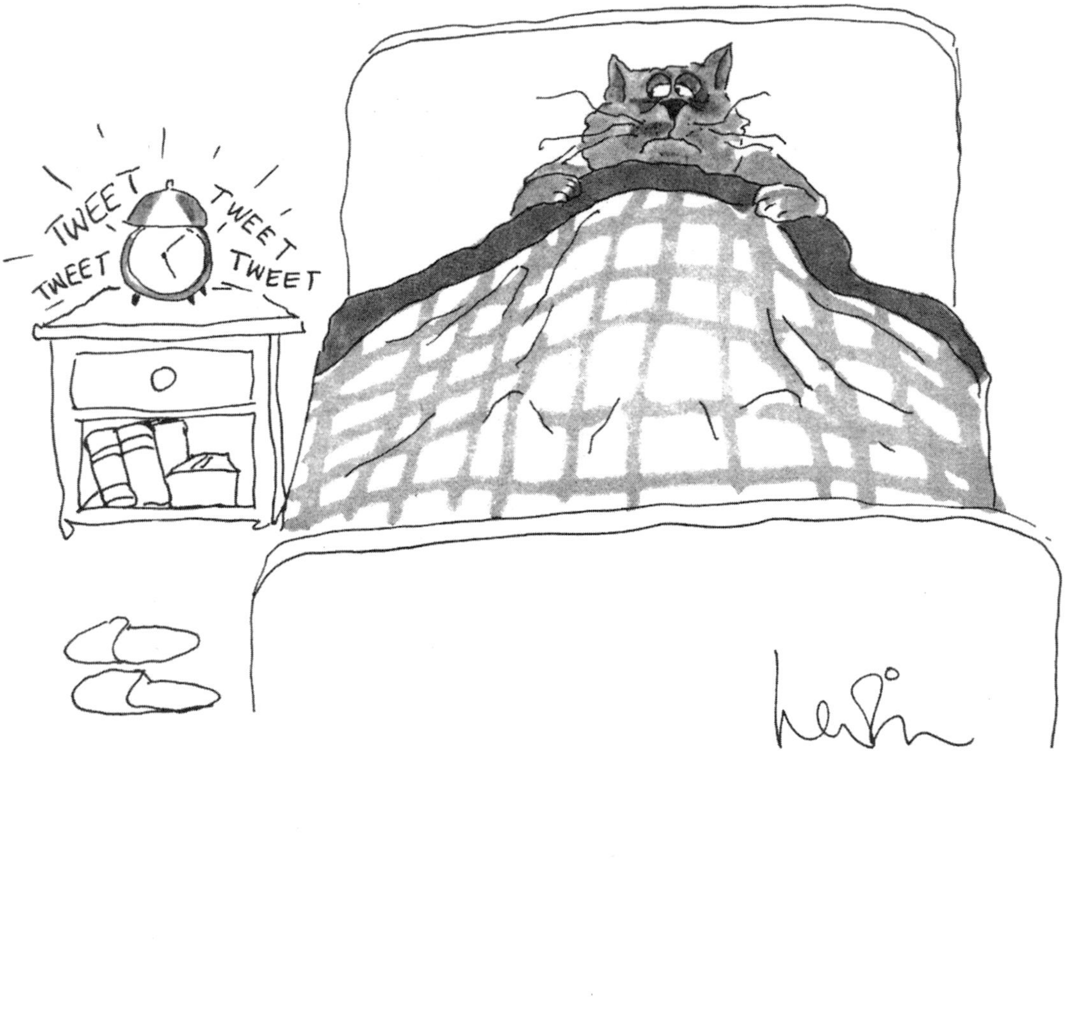
TWEET
TWEET
TWEET
TWEET

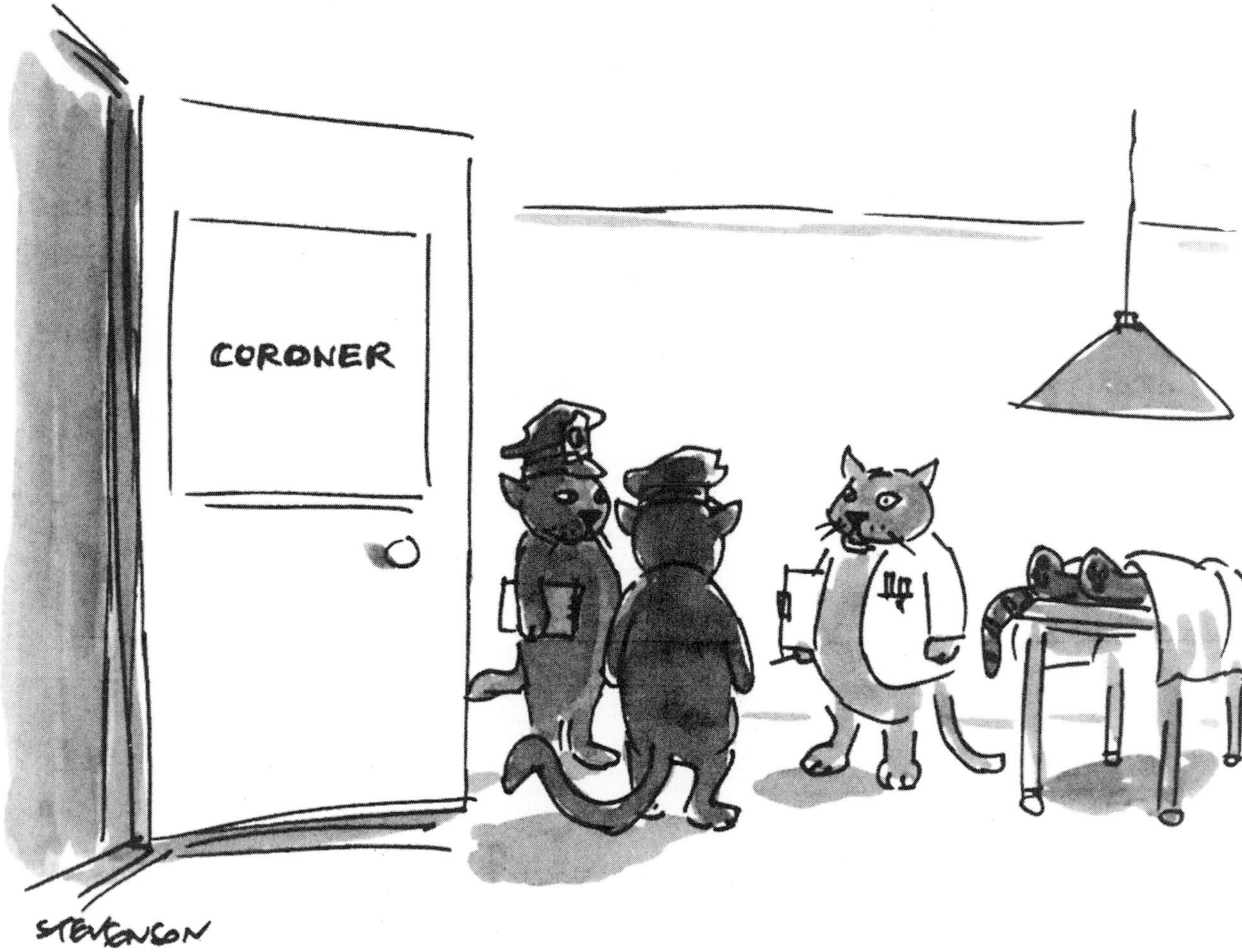
CORONER
STEVENSON

"Curiosity."

"We had the usual exchange of gifts—she gave me this
diamond collar, and I ate all my dinner."

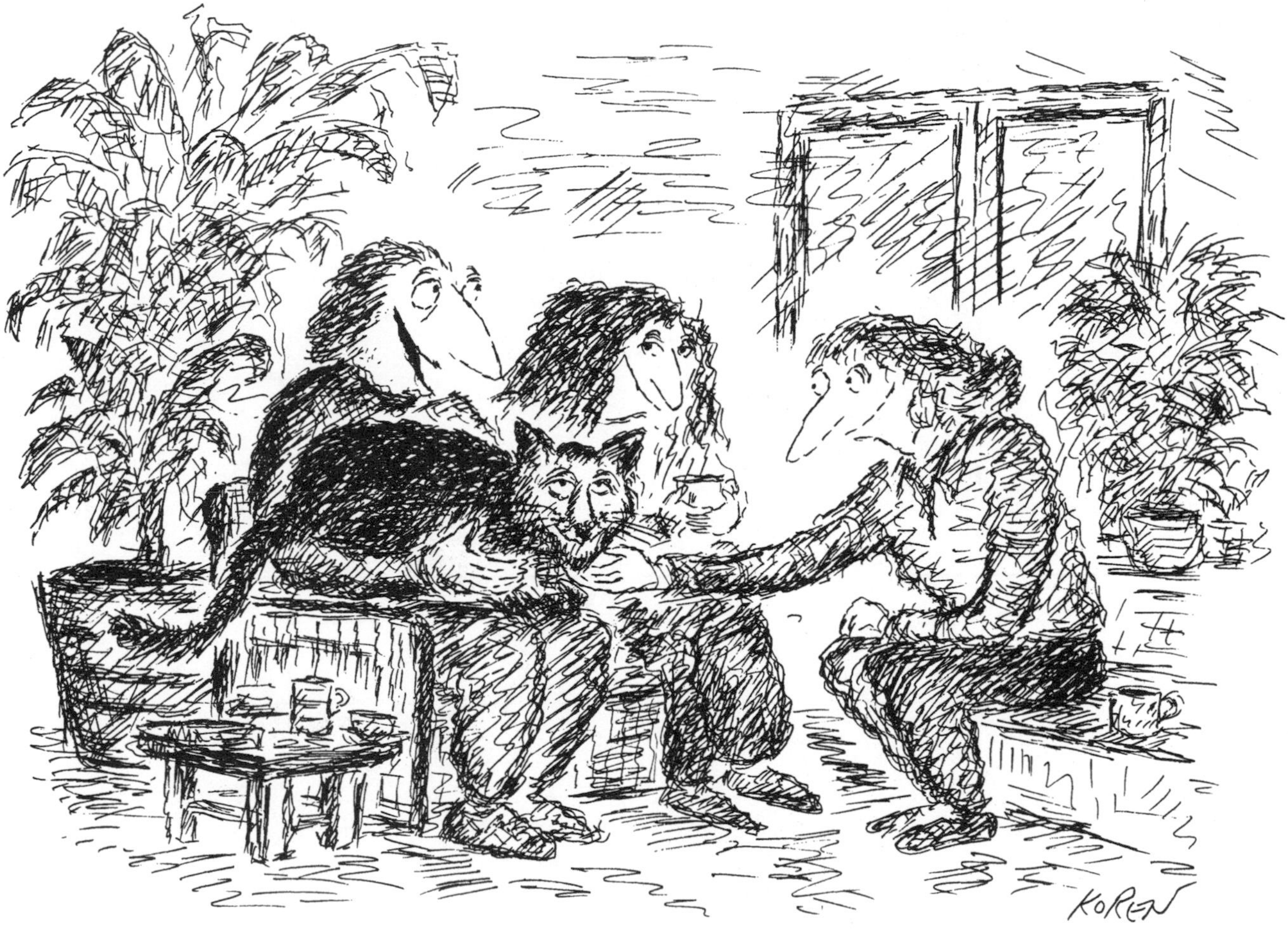
KOREN

"She turned fourteen years old this week,
but we think she's ageless."

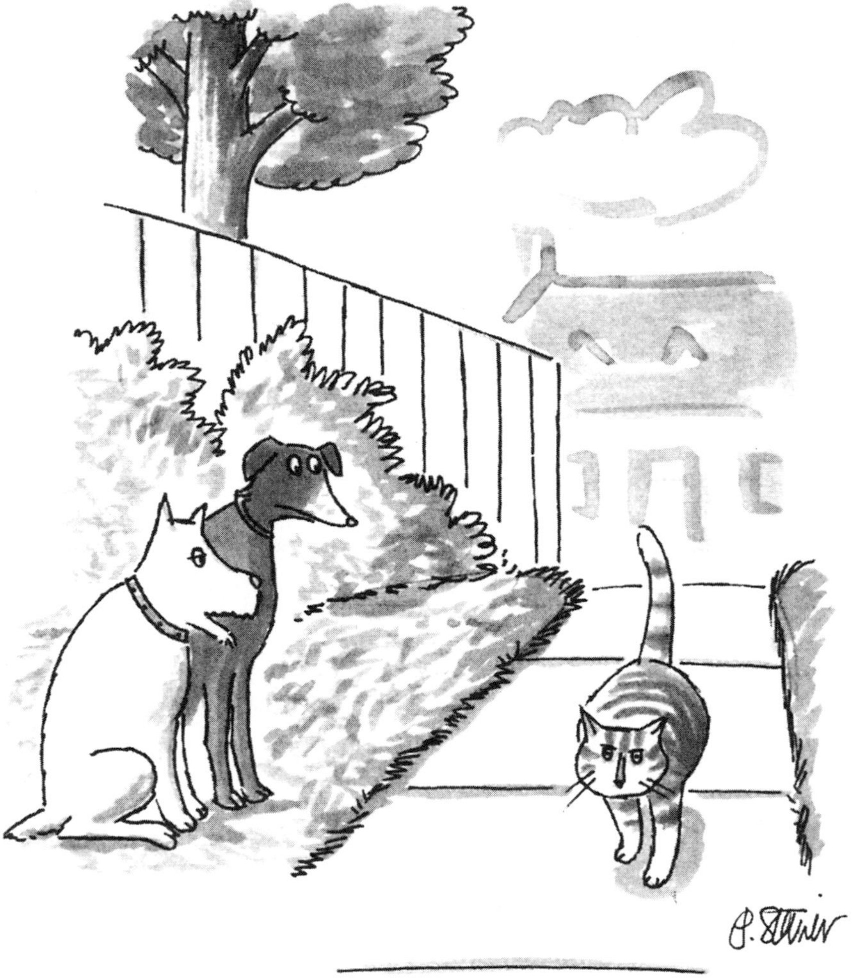
P. Steiner

"Are we talking about life style or orientation?"

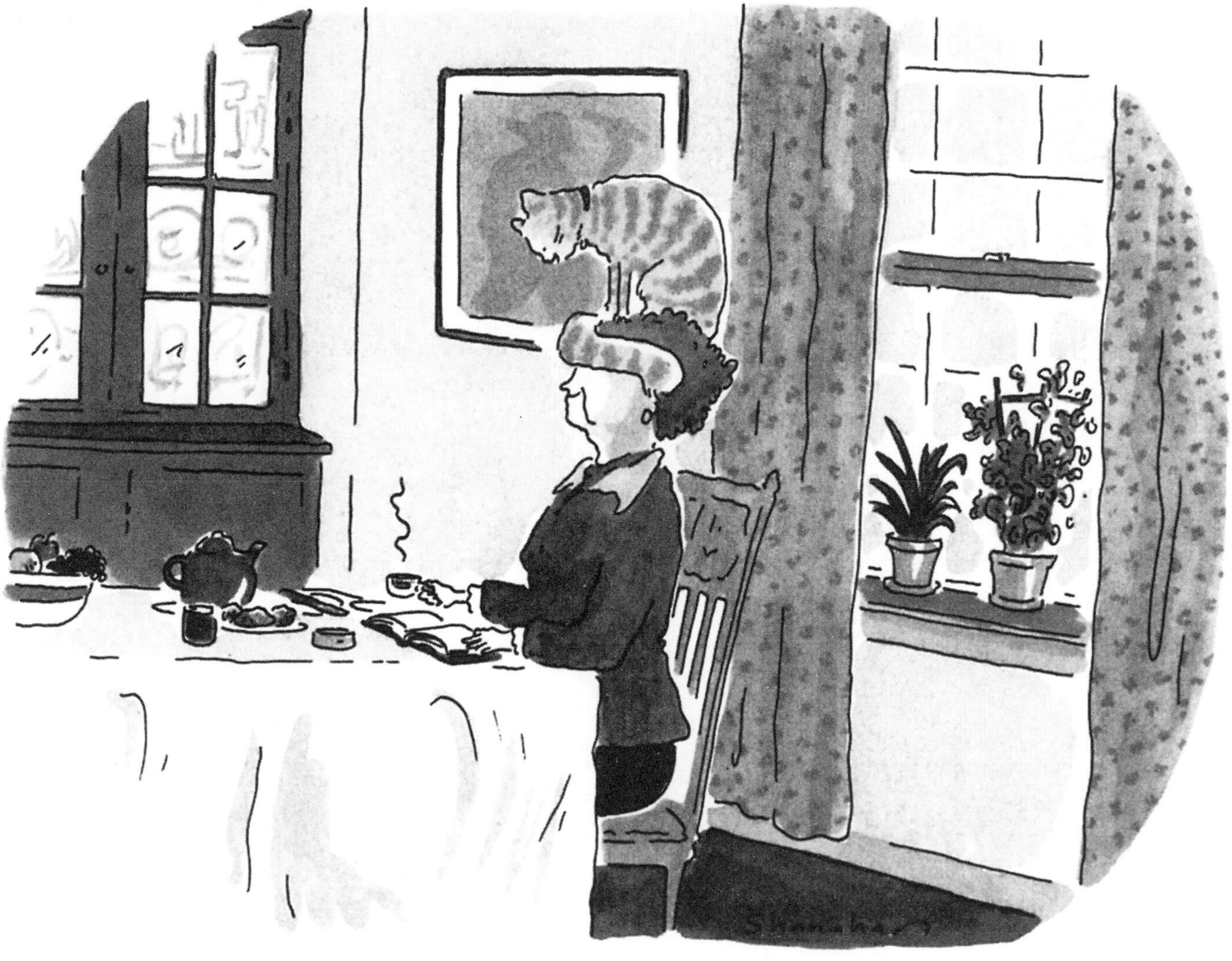

"Guess who?"

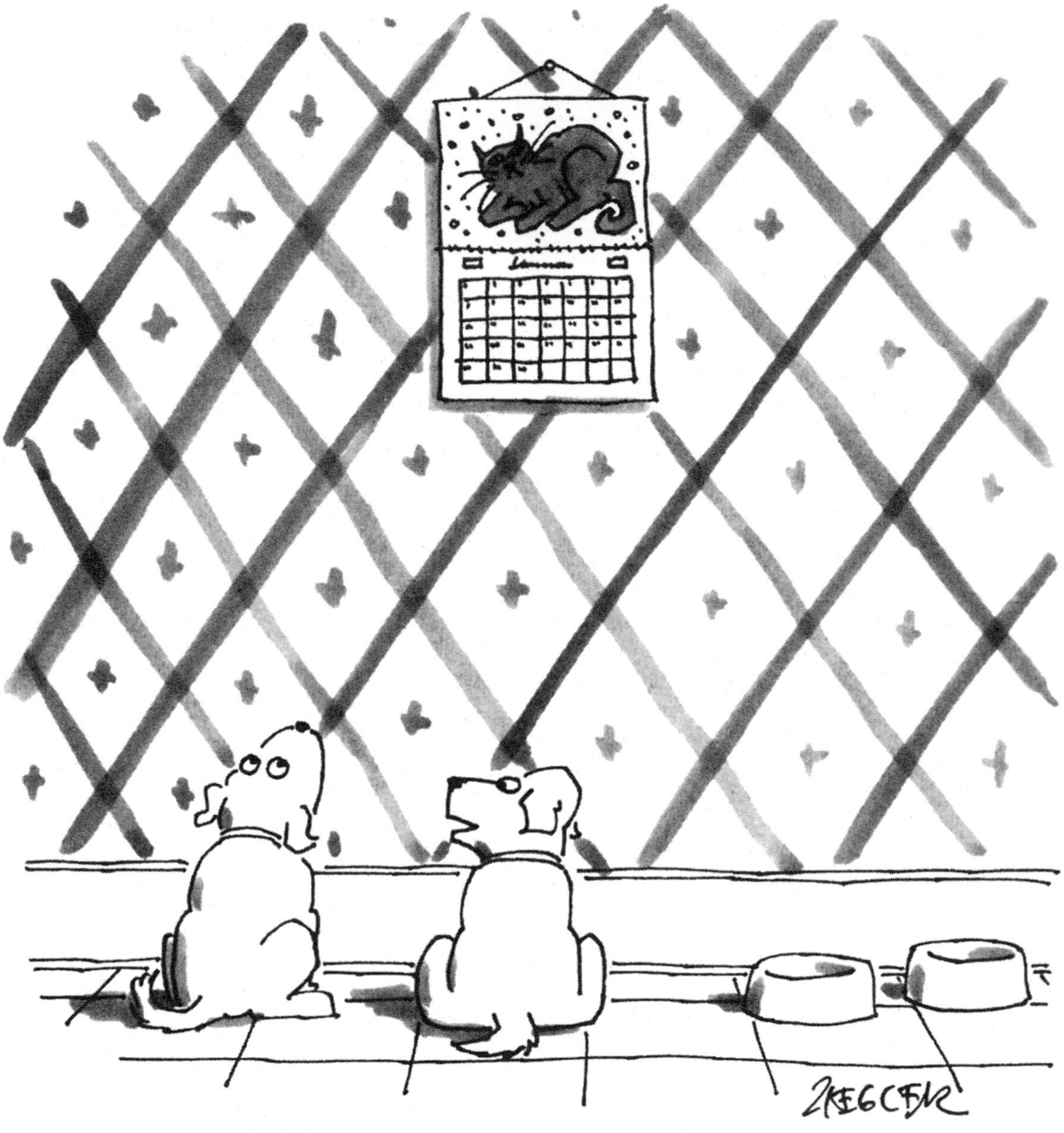

"It's a cat calendar, so it may not be all that accurate."

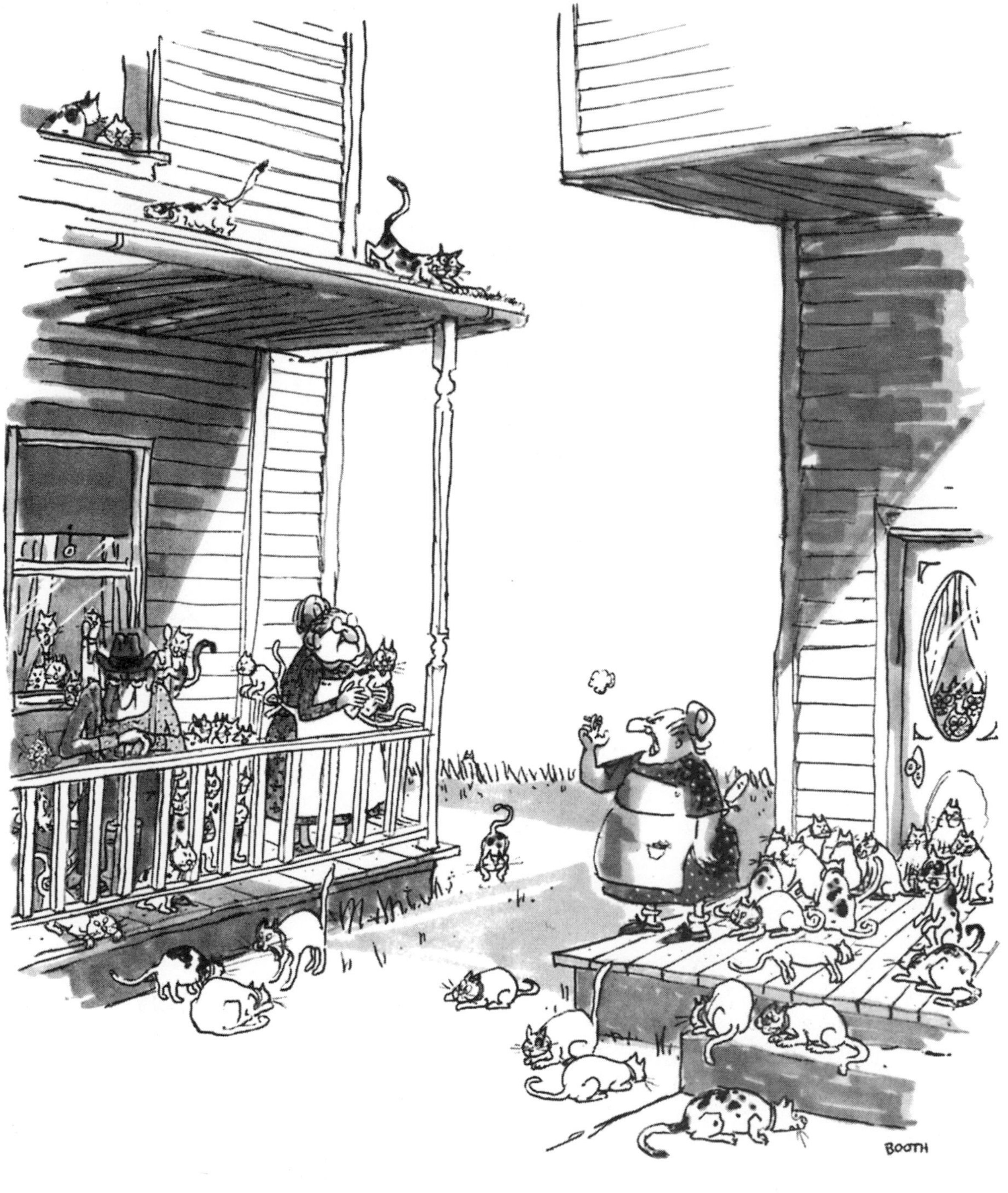
BOOTH

"I'll give you three cans of Happy Herds Condensed Milk for two cans of Affaire de Coeur Flaky Salmon."

"There's no need for your kitty to be envious. After state and federal taxes and legal and administrative fees, Chessy's share of Aunt Martha's estate came to hardly anything."

"I've been wondering if there isn't some way <u>we</u> could capitalize on the cat craze."

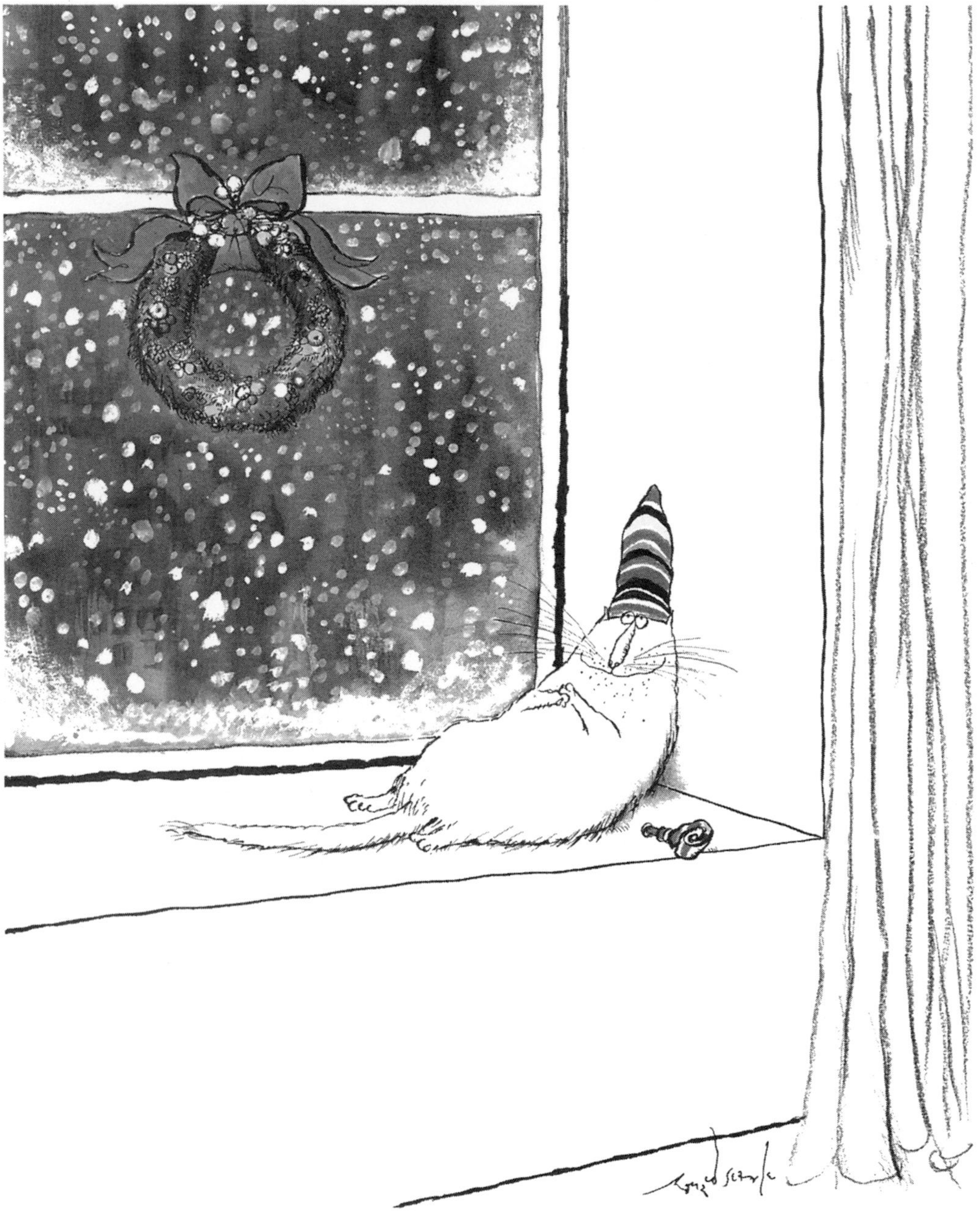